MW01296542

ONLINE

INVESTIGATIONS: Facebook

CI Publishing derives material from active-duty law enforcement officers and instructors with years of experience in the subject matter. The authors of ONLINE INVESTIGATIONS: Facebook chose to remain anonymous as they are prevented from disclosing their identities for operational security reasons and due to departmental policies regarding attribution and endorsements.

FIRST EDITION

CI PUBLISHING

Books may be purchased in bulk or using a government purchase order by contacting the publisher at:

CI Publishing
4695 Chabot Drive Suite 200, Pleasanton, CA 94588
Publisher: CI Publishing
Editor: Elizabeth Peterson
1. Law Enforcement 2. Investigations 3. Social Media
First Edition
Printed in the United States of America

Contents

INTRODUCTION

Facebook is the elephant in the room when it comes to crime and social networking. It is the largest and most popular social network site in the world, with over 1 billion active monthly users—that's roughly one in seven people on the planet. Of these users, 757 million people use Facebook on a daily basis. 945 million people use Facebook on a mobile device with 556 million doing do on a daily basis.

Facebook can be used as a messaging service, social media, and as a sign in for other services

With statistics like that, it's easy to see how Facebook could attract an array of criminal activity. The site and services have been used for cyber bullying, enticement and sexual exploitation of minors, and as a platform for gangs and other organized criminal groups.

Using Facebook as an investigative tool, does not require advanced training or expensive software. It simply takes patience while allowing the company to comply with legal process, a willingness to follow the steps needed to effectively investigate these types of cases, and the knowledge provided in this book.

How This Book Is Written

I wrote this book with two levels in mind; the first geared towards the patrol officer and the second level aimed more at the sophisticated investigator. First, I will walk you the basic steps of navigating the publically available Facebook pages to garner information about potential suspects, crime data, capturing images and various content and flagging it as evidence. Then, as the book continues, I will walk you through more sophisticated techniques used to work with the company when the information you need cannot be obtained with a basic Google search and some surface-level Facebook trolling. We'll outline how and when to write legal demands, such as warrants and subpoenas. I will also provide you with language you can use in all of these cases. Finally, I will discuss how to develop viable leads based on information you received from Facebook after a legal demand is served.

Information Generally Available to You on Facebook

Facebook accounts are comprised of many constantly evolving parts, which are usually updated on a moment-by-moment basis. During an investigation, it is important to understand how all of the parts work together, how they are updated, and what user information and data these moving parts store. It is also important to remember that the information can easily be deleted or changed by the user, at any time during your investigation.

Understanding the Components and Naming Conventions of Facebook Accounts

In this section, we will review all of the parts and collected data on a user's Facebook page, these are also known as data types. They represent all of the information a user could have on their Facebook account, all of which is retained by the company. This data is not only entered by the user but then also modified by friends associated with the account, and evolves over time as Facebook acquires and analyzes more information from the account user's activity. If you are monitoring a public account, many of the following data fields in this list will be available to you. It is current as of the publication date of this book.

About Me

This section contains information the user added to the About section of their timeline. It may include information such as relationships and relationship status, word and education history, and the subject's residence or location. This section includes any updates or changes the user made in the past and what is currently listed in the about section of their timeline.

Account History Status

This lists the dates when the account was activated, re-activated, deactivated, disabled, and/or deleted.

Account Closure Date	Account Still Active	true

Active Sections

Consists of all stored active sessions, including the date, time, device, Internet Protocol (IP) address, cookie information, and the type of browser used to access Facebook.

Ads Clicked

Displays the dates, times, and titles of Facebook Ads clicked. This information is only retained for a very short amount of time but the exact duration is not specified by Facebook.

Address

The user's current address or any past addresses they have associated with their account.

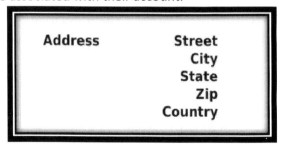

Address	Street
	City
	State
	Zip
	Country

Ad Topics

A list of topics the subject may be interested in and targeted by Facebook. This is based on the user's stated likes, interests, and other data they include in their Timeline.

Alternate Name
If the user has any alternate names, such as maiden name, nickname, or moniker, this information will be included in this section.

Apps
All of the applications the users added to their Facebook account. This area is often overlooked by many investigators and can provide critical information. Users may download apps for games, photos, and videos, but they can also install applications for communication and video conferencing such as Skype.

Birthday Visibility
Whether a user's birthdate is visible in their Timeline.

Chat History
This includes a history of the conversations a user has had on Facebook Chat. If a user deletes their chat history and messages the same information may still be available from the person they were communicating with providing they have not also deleted it.

Check-ins
A listing of the locations a user has checked into using Facebook.

Connections
Includes a list of other Facebook users who have liked the user's page or place, RSVP'd to an event, installed their

application, or checked into an advertised place within 24 hours of viewing or clicking on an ad or Sponsored Story.

Credit Cards
If the user has made purchases on Facebook, such as applications, as has provided Facebook a credit card number this information will be listed here.

Currency
The user's preferred currency on Facebook. If they use Facebook Payments, this will be used to display prices and charge credit cards.

Current City
The user's city they added to the About section of their Timeline.

Date of Birth
The date of birth the user added to Birthday in the About section of their timeline.

Deleted Friends
A list of other Facebook users who have been removed as friends by the user.

6

Education

Any information the user added to the Education field in the About section of their Timeline.

Emails

Email addresses added to the user's account. This includes those that have been removed by the user.

Events

Events the user has been invited to or joined.

Facial Recognition Data

Facebook assigns a unique number based on a comparison of the photos they've been tagged in. This information may assist investigators in identifying images in other Facebook accounts where the subject has been tagged.

Family

Friends who the user has indicated are family members.

Favorite Quotes

Information the user added to their Favorite Quotes section of the About section in their Timeline.

Followers

A list of other Facebook users who follow the user.

Following
A list of people who the user follows.

Friend Requests
Pending sent and received friend requests.

Friends
A list of the user's Facebook friends. This includes the Facebook ID number and the name listed on the friends' account.

Gender
The gender the user added to the About section of their Timeline.

Groups
A list of groups the user belongs to on Facebook.

Hidden from News Feed

Any Facebook friends, applications, or pages the user has hidden from their News Feed.

Hometown

The place the user identified as their hometown in the About section of their Timeline.

IP Addresses

A list of the Internet Protocol (IP) addresses where the user has logged into their Facebook account. This may not include all historical IP addresses as Facebook deletes them according to a retention schedule they have not disclosed. However, in some cases, IP addresses appear to have been retained since the Facebook account was opened.

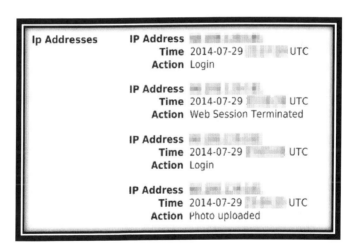

Last Location

The last location associated with a user updates.

Likes on Others' Posts

Posts, photos, or other content the user has liked.

Like on Your Posts from Others

Likes on the user's posts, photos, or other content.

Like on Other Sites

Likes the user has made on sites off of Facebook.

Linked Accounts

A list of the accounts the user has linked to their Facebook account. This information may be incredibly important as it reveals other applications and services where the user created an account using their Facebook profile. This may include communications services and other social networking sites.

Locale

The language the user selected to view Facebook in.

Logins

The Internet Protocol (IP) address, date, and time associated with logins to the user's Facebook account.

Logouts

The Internet Protocol (IP) address, date, and time associated with logouts to the user's Facebook account.

Messages

Messages the user has sent and received on Facebook. Deleted messages are not retained. However, it may be possible to recover the message from the Facebook account of the other user the suspect was in contact with.

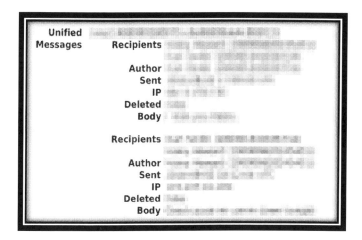

Name
The name on the user's Facebook account.

Name Changes
Any changes the user has made to the original name used to sign up for Facebook.

Networks
Affiliations with schools or employers the user belongs to on Facebook.

Notes

11

Any notes the user has written and published to their account.

Notification Settings
A list of all user notification preferences such as email and/or SMS text messaging.

Pages You Admin
A list of pages the user is the administrator for.

Pending Friend Requests
Pending sent and received Facebook friend requests.

Phone Numbers
All mobile phone numbers the user added to their account. This includes verified phone numbers the user added for security purposes.

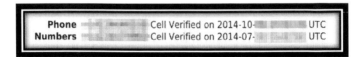

Photos
Digital images uploaded to the user's account

Photos Metadata
Any EXIF or metadata transmitted with a user's uploaded digital images.

Physical Token
Badges a user has added to their account.

Pokes

A list of who the user has poked and who poked them. Pokes from the Facebook mobile application are not included. After the recipient has viewed the content it is permanently deleted from Facebook's system.

Political Views

Any information the user added to Political Views in the About section of their Timeline.

Posts by You

Anything the user posted to their own Timeline, including photos, videos, and status updates.

Posts by Others

Anything posted to the user's Timeline by someone else, including wall posts or links shared on their Timeline by friends.

Posts to Other

Anything the user posted to another user's Timeline, including photos, videos, and status updates.

Privacy Settings

The user's privacy settings; whether their profile is public or private.

Recent Activities

13

Actions and interactions the user has recent had with other Facebook users.

Registration Date
The date the user created their Facebook account.

Religious Views
The current information the user added to the Religious Views in the About section of their timeline.

Removed Friends
A list of those removed by the user as a friend.

Screen
Associated screen names added by the user to their account and the services they are associated to. These screen names may be hidden or visible on the user's account.

Searches
The user's Facebook search history.

Shares
Content, such as a news article or webpage, the user shared with others on Facebook using the Share button or link. Along with the file, Facebook retains the file name, the link to the file, the IP address the file was

shared from, some EXIF/metadata, and any comments made by other Facebook users.

Other data may include 'tags' by the user or other Facebook users regarding the identity or location of the subject or subjects in the image.

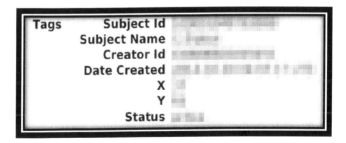

Images may also contain the GPS coordinates where they were taken.

15

Camera Make	LG Electronics
Camera Model	VS660
Orientation	0
Original Width	720
Original Height	0
Exposure	
Fstop	
Iso Speed	0
Focal Length	431/100
Latitude	34 ▓▓▓▓▓▓▓
Longitude	-85 ▓▓▓▓▓▓
Tags	

Spoken Languages

The language the user added to Spoke Languages in the About section of their timeline.

Status Updates

Any status updates the user has posted, including if the update came from a mobile device and any comments by other Facebook users.

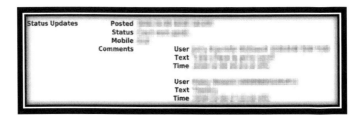

Work

The current employment information added by the user to Work in the About section of their timeline.

16

Vanity URL

The user's Facebook Uniform Resource Locator; usually their username or vanity name for the account.)

Videos

Videos the user has posted to their timeline.

Metadata Field Descriptions

The following information is not available to the casual user but shows up in the results Facebook sends back to the investigating officer.

Facebook pictures, videos, messages, and posting have various metadata fields associated with them. Metadata is data that describes other data. Facebook metadata fields may include:

Uri	Unified resource identifier of the item
fb_item_type	Identifies item type such as Wallitem, Newsitem, or Photo
parent_item-num	Parent item number. Sub items are tracked to parent
thread_id	Unique identifier of a message thread
recipients	All recipients of a message listed by name
recipients_id	All recipients of a message listed by user id
album_id	Unique id number of a photo or video item
post_id	Unique id number of a wall post
application	Application used to post to Facebook (e.g., from an iPhone or other application)
user_img	URL where user profile image is located
user_id	Facebook ID of the poster/author of a Facebook item
account_id	Facebook ID of a user's account
user_name	Display name of poster/author of a Facebook item
created_time	The time a post or message was created
up-dated_time	The time a post or message was revised/updated
To	Name of user whom a wall post is directed to

to_id	Unique ID of user whom a wall post is directed to
Link	URL of any included links
com-ments_num	Number of comments to a post
picture_url	URL where picture is located

Information Facebook Cannot Provide

There are some items that Facebook simply cannot provide you, even if you attempted to serve them a warrant or subpoena. The following things are strictly a no-go.

User's Password

Facebook is unable to provide law enforcement officers with a user's password even with a court order directing them to provide the information. Facebook is not intentionally resisting the will of the court or deliberately obstructing a law enforcement investigation. The simple fact is that passwords are encrypted and stored in such a fashion that they are unreadable by the very company that stores them.

Deleted Data

When it comes to Facebook, deleted means deleted. Once the wall post, picture, video, message, or profile is deleted by the user it is gone. There are no backup copies, tapes, or archives retained by the company. Facebook's deletion practices are the reason immediately preserving evidence on the service is so important. We will discuss the best ways to accomplish this in "Chapter 3: Preserving Facebook Pages as Evidence."

Deactivated Accounts

However, just because a Facebook account is no longer visible does not mean it no longer exists. Users have a choice to delete or deactivate an account.

A user many choose to deactivate their account instead of deleting their entire profile. A deactivated account is no longer visible to anyone searching for it. However, Facebook retains deactivated profiles, and all associated data, indefinitely.

Deleted Versus Deactivated

Facebook will not disclose whether an account has been deleted or deactivated without legal process. Nevertheless, there is still a way to determine if an invisible account still has information that can be recovered by law enforcement officers.

To ascertain whether an account is deleted or deactivated, submit a preservation request using the Law Enforcement Records Online Service (LEROS.) When a preservation letter is submitted through the system a deleted account will result in no records being found. A deactivated account, even though it is no longer viewable, will still be preserved using LEROS. If the data is preserved in LEROS using the preservation request there is still available data.

Chapter 2: Properly Identifying the Suspect's Facebook Profile

Investigating cases involving Facebook relies heavily on properly identifying the suspect's profile. Many criminals are savvy enough to use false identities so digging little deeper is usually required. Using a suspect's real name or the name on their profile page may not return the proper results. Using vague or non-descriptive profile identifiers will also fail to locate the correct profile. For example, if a law enforcement officer submits a legal demand for an 'Unknown' account, the response from Facebook will be for the 2011 Liam Neesom movie "Unknown."

Similarly, using the name on the Facebook page will also lead to incorrect results. For example, the Facebook page of the Honolulu Police Department lists the page name as such. However, this is not the correct identification for the organization's Facebook page.

Vanity URLs

Vanity URLs, a unique web address that is branded for marketing purposes, are becoming more common. They are a type of custom URL that exists to help users remember and find a specific page of your website or page on a social media site. Because vanity URLs are designed to be easy to remember they are often just as easily misconstrued. The uniform resource locator (URL) displayed in a web browser shows what Facebook calls the 'Vanity URL.' This is the correct identification for the profile page. If the Honolulu Police Department's Facebook page was the target of the investigation, legal process would identify the profile as honolulu.police and not Honolulu Police Department.

Locating a Facebook ID

Facebook assigns all profiles a numeric identifier. However, this identifier is not easily located on the profile page. An easy way to translate a Vanity URL into a User ID number is to copy the URL and paste it into www.whatismyfacebookid.com.

Select **Lookup numeric ID...** and the website will translate the Vanity URL into the User ID number.

Finding the Facebook ID Using a Mobile Device

Locating a User ID from within a mobile application is relatively simple and can be done even if the Facebook account is private. Locate and select the **About** button.

Select the **About** button from the menu.

The results will display the user name required for submitting a legal demand for the proper Facebook account.

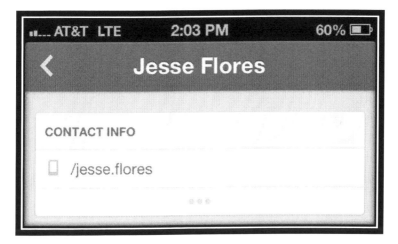

Using an Email Address to Verify an Account

Facebook can search their records for to help you identify a suspect's Facebook page based on the user's email address. Only one Facebook profile can be associated with an email account. A user with multiple Facebook accounts will necessarily have multiple email accounts.

Facebook may be able to determine other mobile phones, tablets, and computer that have logged in to different profiles but use the same Internet Protocol (IP) address. This may be a beneficial item to include in a legal demand as it may reveal other Facebook profiles the suspect is using or has used. Shockingly, many criminals may take the time to use multiple Facebook accounts with false information. Directing Facebook, via legal process, to check if an IP address is associated with additional profiles may show these additional accounts.

Checking Facebook accounts by IP address requires knowing the IP address the suspect used or uses. While many IP addresses are fixed, others are not. Also, some cellular service providers have a limited pool of IP addresses that are used simultaneously. The results of a legal demand for a mobile IP address can reveal hundreds or thousands of users.

For a detailed examination of IP addresses, how to obtain them, and how to investigate them, see the subsequent section entitled IP addresses.

Chapter 3: Preserving Facebook Pages as Evidence

Because Facebook is a constantly changing and evolving social site, a critical component to investigating Facebook is to preserve the evidence when it is located.

There are three main methods for preserving evidence on Facebook:

- Writing and serving preservation letters and requests.
- Capturing images and properly preserving them.
- Using online preservation software tools—these are commercially available software tools and services for preserving images and data content.

Many times a criminal suspect will alter or delete incriminating evidence once they become aware of the law enforcement investigation. Also, the legal process to compel Facebook to relinquish information can be a cumbersome, time-consuming process. The steps an investigating officer takes at the initial stages of the case can determine the outcome of any criminal prosecution. Mastering these methods will and knowing when to employ them will save you a lot time and hassle in the long run.

Submitting Preservation Letters

Your first option is to submit a preservation request, sometimes referred to as a preservation letter. A preservation letter is issued pursuant to Federal law; specifically, Title 18 United States Code 2703(f). The letter is issued on departmental stationary by the requesting officer and does not need to be signed by a magistrate, prosecuting attorney, or supervisor. The letter requests the provider, in this case Facebook, to preserve records associated with an account or user name for 90 days. The preservation letter can be renewed one time for an additional 90 days of preservation. No records or other information will be turned over without a search warrant, court order, or subpoena. A preservation letter cannot be used to proactively secure data on a Facebook profile. It only preserves what is on the profile at the time the letter is received.

Preservation letters should also come with a non-disclosure statement directing Facebook not to divulge the existence of the letter as it would unduly damage the investigation.

Facebook has made it easy to preserve records for a profile. They have created a Law Enforcement Request Online System (LEROS.) LEROS allows investigators to submit a preservation letter electronically. No physical letter needs to be delivered to the company. LEROS is also used to submit legal demands such as search warrants, court orders, and subpoenas. These can be scanned and sent via the LEROS system.

To preserve a Facebook profile go to https://www.facebook.com/records.

New users can request access by submitting a law enforcement email address and the security check.

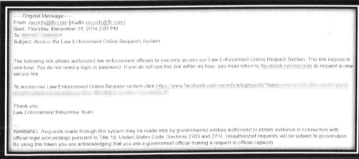

Using a preservation letter request will show if there is information, if a preservation letter is sent and "No Account Found" then there is no information available whatsoever

Once an account has been created a preservation letter can be submitted electronically. Preservation letters require the Facebook User ID, the Uniform Resource Locator, or the user's email address.

Data and Image Capturing

The second method for preserving evidence found on Facebook is to capture the images and data as they are displayed on the profile page. The simplest method is to use a screen capture such as by hitting the print screen button or creating a PDF file. However, there are several evidence and chain of custody issues involved in simply printing the screen. There is little to prevent a defense attorney from arguing the image was later altered or tampered with by law enforcement officers. While it is unlikely a law enforcement officer is going to risk their honor and their livelihood by using an image editor to try and incriminate a suspect, it only takes doubt in the minds of one juror to lose a case.

Image Preservation the Right Way

Most law enforcement officers investigating Facebook will take a screen shot or print a PDF of the profile and later book those images into evidence on a CD or DVD. More needs to be done to limit the opportunity to a defense attorney to raise reasonable doubt regarding the evidence and the chain of custody.

The first step is to create a screen capture that includes the image or data to be preserved, the profile site where the data was obtained from, the date, time, and officer who viewed the Facebook page, and indicators of evidence tampering. All of these functions can be done with the use of free software.

It is important to address the technical aspects of installing these programs before detailing the steps of using them. Many law enforcement officers work at agencies where they are not permitted to install outside software on a departmental computer. These same officers are trusted by their departments with a baton, Taser®, chemical agents, a sidearm, a shotgun or rifle, and the ability to detain and arrest people but they are not trustworthy enough to install software on a computer. This is especially true in larger agencies where the information technology/services department is run by non-law enforcement officers who are only concerned about the possible introduction of a virus into 'their' system and not identifying and arresting criminals. To combat this problem, all of the software discussed is portable. This means it can be downloaded and copied onto a USB drive and run from it. The software does not need to be installed to operate.

CORE SKILL: Using Screen Capture Software

There are a number of free and paid screen capture software but ShareX is one of the best available. The steps to set it up the first time might seem unnecessarily complicated when compared with the simplicity of hitting the print screen button. But the resulting images will help establish a chain of custody and make for better investigations and prosecution. ShareX can be downloaded from https://getsharex.com/. The portable version of the software can be downloaded for free from the website http://www.softpedia.com/get/PORTABLE-SOFTWARE/Multimedia/Graphics/ShareX-Portable.shtml. Both sites are trustworthy but all files, not just those discussed in this manual, should be checked with a virus detection program before they are installed and used. A free alternative to the virus detection software installed by a department is https://www.virustotal.com/. Virustotal.com uses 40 different virus and malware detection services to scan a file and determine if there are any unwanted surprises hidden in the code.

ShareX will download as a .ZIP file. This file will need to be un-packed to work. Law enforcement officers who do not have an unzipping program can download 7-Zip from http://www.7-zip.org/. 7-Zip is free and also portable so it does not need to be installed on an agency's computer.

Once the ShareX file has been unzipped it can be launched by clicking the icon.

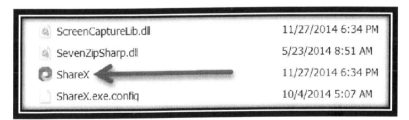

The program will open into the main interface screen.

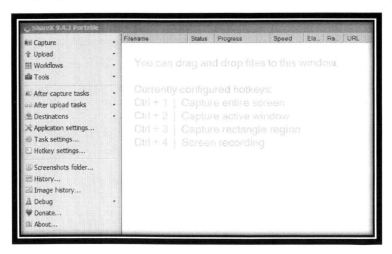

The first step is to configure the capture keys.

There are four capture combinations:

- Capture entire screen
- Capture active window
- Capture rectangle region
- Screen recording

By default, ShareX will attempt to register hotkeys to activate the specific functions. In some cases, the default hotkeys ShareX wants to use may be in use for other programs or functions. If the box is green the buttons are available to use.

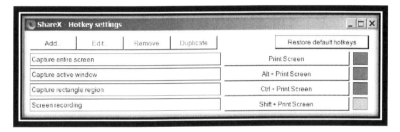

If the box is red it means another software program is already using those keys and they cannot be used to control ShareX. Custom hotkeys can be created by clicking on the box with the unavailable hotkey. The box will change to a green colored box that reads **Select a hotkey...**

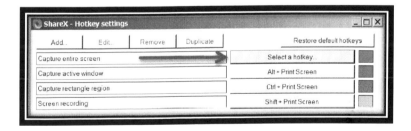

Use any desired key, or combination of keys to assign a function to a hotkey. In this example the Control button and the numbers one to four have been used to assign a function to a hotkey.

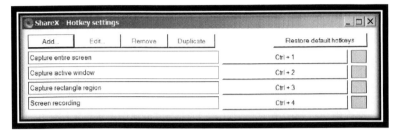

By default, ShareX will place all captured screen images into a folder within the ShareX file called Screenshots. If ShareX is being run from as a portable application it would make sense to keep the files with the program. However, if the program is being run from a desktop or the pictures need to be saved in another location, the destination folder can be changed. From the main menu select **Application Settings**.

36

Select the **Paths** tab at the top. Use the **Browse** button to navigate to the desired destination folder.

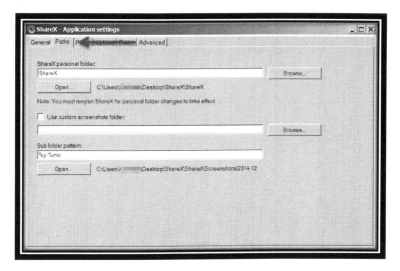

By default ShareX will create a .GIF file format of any screen capture taken. Some agencies prefer their images to be in .JPG format. The screen capture output in ShareX can be changed by going to **Task Settings** from the main menu.

Select the **Image** tab at the top of the page and change the file type and resolution desired.

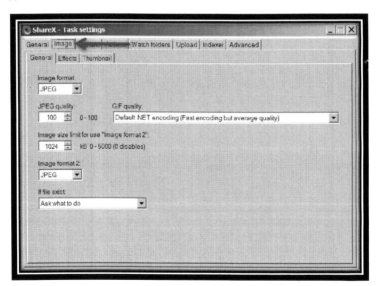

At this point it is possible to begin taking screen captures of Facebook profile pages. However, there are additional options within ShareX that can be used to assist with establishing chain of custody. Specifically, it is possible to put a date time stamp on the image, as well as, additional information such as a report or incident number and investigator name. From the main menu select **Task Settings** and then **Image**.

From the **Images** tab select the **Effects** subtab and then **Image effects configuration**.

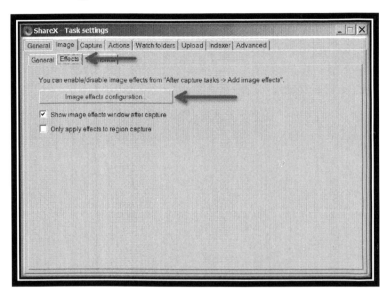

The resulting window should appear similar to the one below.

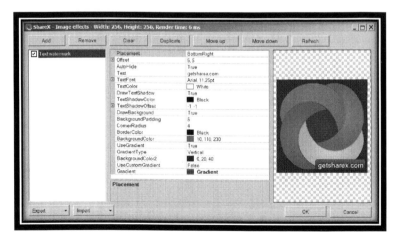

To automatically place the date and time the image was taken it will be necessary to format the data in the **Text** field. Clicking on the box with three dots brings up a menu of the codes needed to place the desired information in the image. For example to place the date and time the picture was taken, replace the data in the **Text** field with %mo/%d/%y %h:%mi:%s. The slashes separate the month, day, and year and the colons separate the hours, minutes, and seconds. There is a space between year and hour to keep the da ta from running together.

Make sure to select **OK**. Now, when an image is captured using ShareX, the date and time it was taken will be placed on the picture.

By default the first set of data will be in the bottom right of the screen capture. To change the location select the **Placement** field and use the drop down arrow to navigate to the area where the data should be placed on the image. The boxes in the drop down menu correspond to the area on the image where the data will be placed. For example, selecting the bottom right box will place the data in the lower right of the image. Selecting the bottom left box will place the data in the lower left of the image.

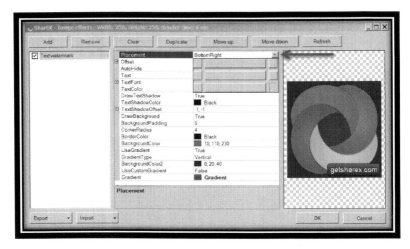

Additional data may be placed on the image such as the investigators name and/or the case number. To add these fields go back to **Image effects configuration** and then select **Add** from the upper menu. This will bring up additional options. **Select Drawings** and then **Text Watermark**.

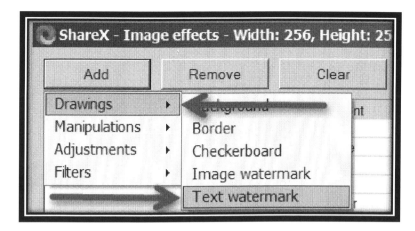

Change the placement to **BottomCenter** and replace the **Text** with whatever additional information should appear in the image.

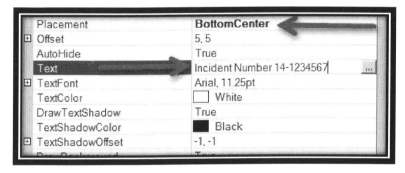

Additional information can be added such as the investigator's name and agency by repeating the process. Additional data can be placed in the **BottomLeft**.

Resulting screen captures will have the data automatically stamped on the lower portion of the image.

ShareX has addition functions that can be configured automatically. For example, screen captures can be automatically saved into a clipboard and pasted directly into a document or report without going back to the file where the images are saved.

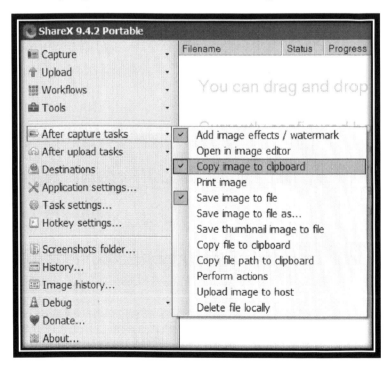

CORE SKILL: Maintaining the Integrity of Digital Evidence

As discussed previously proving a digital image, such as a screen capture, can be important during the prosecution of a suspect. It is critical to take an additional step to preserve the integrity of images because the screen captures taken by a law enforcement officer during the investigation may be the only evidence that remains if a suspect deletes their profile or removes an image or comment.

Understanding and Using Hash Functions

The process of maintaining the integrity of digital evidence is best accomplished by showing the file was not changed or altered after it was viewed or seized. The computer forensics field has long used hash functions or hash algorithms to show a file is the original. A hash function is an algorithm applied to a file that calculates a unique sequence of letters and/or numbers. Any changes to the underlying file are revealed when the same algorithm is applied. Even small alterations to a file are revealed as changes to the hash value. For example, the calculation of the sentence

45

"The quick brown fox jumps over the lazy dog." has value of 408d94384216f890ff7a0c3528e8bed1e0b01621 using the SHA1 hash algorithm.

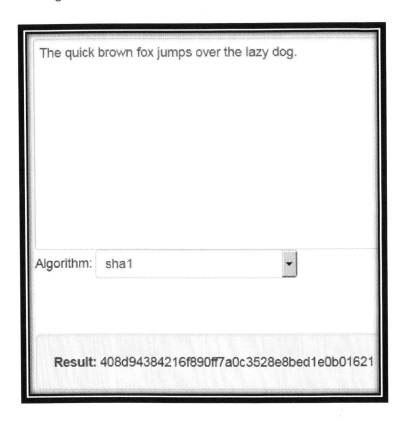

The same sentence with the period removed has a SHA1 hash value of 2fd4e1c67a2d28fced849ee1bb76e7391b93eb12.

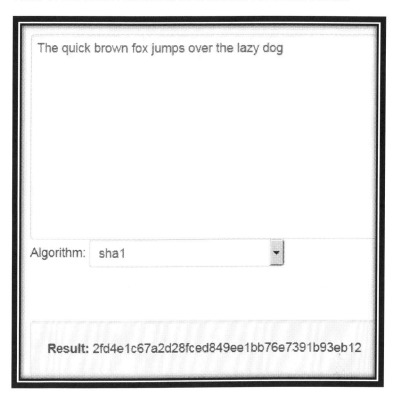

The quick brown fox jumps over the lazy dog

Algorithm: sha1

Result: 2fd4e1c67a2d28fced849ee1bb76e7391b93eb12

Changing the characteristics of an image file, such a screen capture of a Facebook profile, would be obvious as the hash value would be significant different.

Hash functions come in a number of different variations based on the algorithm used to calculate the properties of a file. Some of the variations of hash functions include MD5, SHA1, SHA256, SHA512, RIPEMD256, Whirlpool, Tiger, CRC, and HAVAL. In the example above SHA1 was used. SHA1 stands for Secure Hash Algorithm and was developed by the National Security Agency. It

47

does not matter what software or Internet site is used to calculate the hash function. As long as the same algorithm is applied and the file is unchanged, the value will remain the same.

Hash functions are becoming the standard for verifying digital evidence in the law enforcement field. Hash functions are routinely used in computer forensics and to verify the integrity of video evidence from in-car camera systems, body worn cameras, and some models of the Taser®. Taking the extra step and applying hash functions to screen captures can assist in preserving the integrity of the evidence.

There are numerous free websites calculating hash. However, these services should be avoided for law enforcement purposes. In order for these websites to calculate the hash of a file they must be allowed to access the file. It is highly unlikely these websites are used for anything other than calculating hash. But the possibility remains a defense attorney could challenge the integrity of the evidence after an unknown website 'touched' the file.

Downloadable options are preferred. Unfortunately, the same restrictions that prevent many law enforcement officers from downloading and installing software such as ShareX apply to hash calculators. Fortunately, the solution is the same. There are a number of free portable applications for hash calculators that can be run from a USB drive without installing them.

An example of one is a free portable application called Hash-MyFiles from Nirsoft.net. The application is available at http://www.nirsoft.net/utils/hash_my_files.html. Once the program is downloaded it will need to be unpacked using a file unzipped such as 7-Zip.

Select the HashMyFiles icon to launch the program.

HashMyFiles is not a pretty program nor does it come with much in the way of instructions. However, the program is relatively intuitive and easy to use.

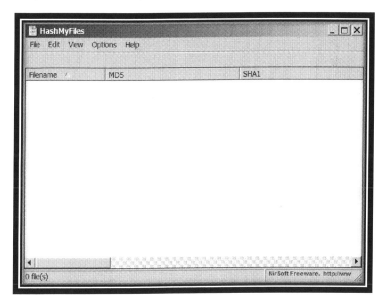

HashMyFiles uses six different popular hash functions including MD5, SHA1, CRC32, SHA-256, SHA-512, and SHA-384. It is always a good idea to use at least two different hash functions. Specific to the MD5 hash function here is evidence that if there were a billion files on a computer and the hash for the files were calculated that two of them would have the same hash value. This is known as a hash collision. To prevent the one in a billion possibility of two files having the same hash many computer security and forensic professionals use at least two hash functions.

Having six different hash values is beyond redundant and unnecessary and they can easily be removed from HashMyFiles by clicking on them.

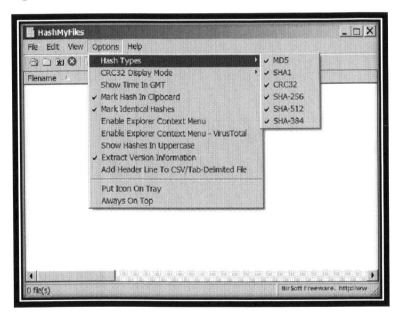

HashMyFiles will display information useful for showing chain of custody and evidence integrity. It will also show information and fields that are not necessarily relevant. The displayed fields can be customized by selecting **View** and **Choose Columns**.

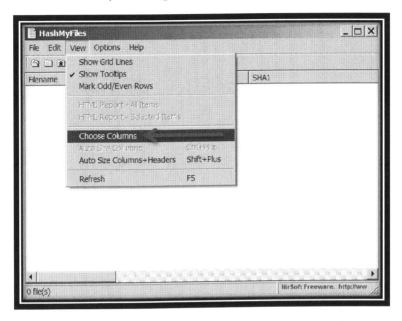

In most cases, it is sufficient to keep the Filename, two hash functions, the full file path name, the modified and created times, and the file size.

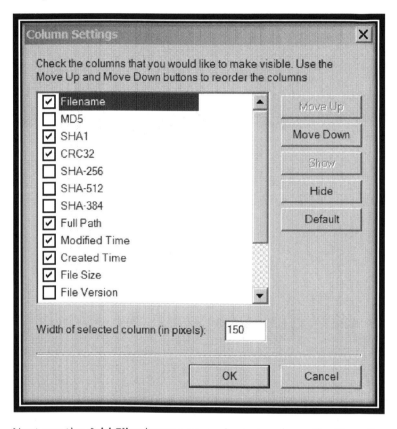

Next use the **Add Files** button to navigate to where the ShareX screen captures have been stored.

Use the **Control** and **A** buttons to select all of the files and then **Open**. All of the screen captures, and their hash values, should be visible in HashMyFiles.

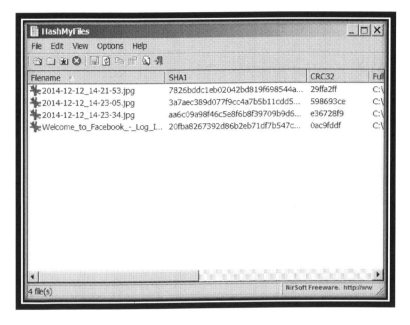

From within HashMyFiles the data can be copied and pasted into a Word document or Excel spreadsheet. However, doing so leaves the column headers off. An alternatives is to select **View** and **HTML Report – All Items**. This creates a HTML webpage with all of the information displayed, including the headers.

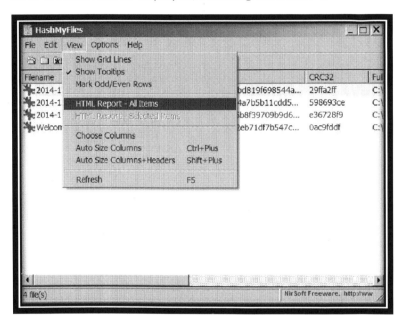

The webpage can be saved for off-line viewing by selecting **File** in the web browser used to open the page and then **Save Page As...**

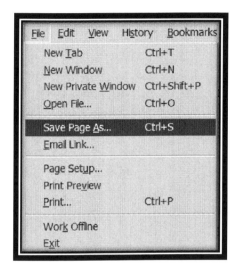

Alternately, the page can be printed by selecting **File** and **Print**. Unfortunately, to print all of the data on a single sheet, the font size becomes extremely small and difficult to read.

Once the hash values of the screen captures have been saved they should be included in the police or incident report and kept as part of the case file. The screen capture images should be booked into evidence using departmental standard operating procedure.

Taking screenshots and hashing files is the recommended method for preserving Facebook evidence. However, downloading the required applications and performing the extra steps are not for everyone, in every situation. Wouldn't it be nice if there was a tool that downloaded all of the publicly available data for you?

Using Preservation Software

Finally, we come to our third method, using downloadable software to preserve evidence found on Facebook. There are commercial software tools and services for preserving and investigating Facebook profiles. These include Internet Evidence Finder from Magnet Forensics and Facebook Forensics from Afentis Forensics. These products have their relative strengths and weakness but share a common problem for many law enforcement investigators-they cost money. Many law enforcement agencies will shell out $200,000 for an armored rescue vehicle without batting an eye but resist spending $50-1,500 to obtain an investigative tool. For the budget impaired law enforcement officer there are a couple of free options in addition to the screen capture method detailed previously.

Facebook Profile Saver

Belkasoft is a computer forensic software development company located in the Russian Federation. One of the tools the company makes freely available is a Facebook Profile Saver. This program allows users to download the photo albums, wall messages consisting of text and images, and the message inbox of a logged in user.   The software can be downloaded from: http://forensic.belkasoft.com/download/bfps/bfps.zip

Facebook Profile Saver makes capturing publicly available information very easy. To begin, enter the Uniform Resource Locator of the Facebook profile under investigation and a destination for the saved files.

Next select the types of data to be saved. Belkasoft's Facebook Profile Saver allows an investigator to save the picture albums and wall messages. However, there are some limitations. The wall albums must be publicly available. Facebook Profile Saver will not locate or save hidden files. Also, the software will not recover wall messages that consist of anything other than text or images. Other file types are not supported. To save messages

57

from the user's Inbox, they must be logged in. Belkasoft Facebook Profile Saver will not recover the Inbox messages of another user's account.

Select the Album, Wall Messages, or Inbox messages and all publicly viewable information will be downloaded and saved.

Belkasoft's Facebook Profile Saver comes with several significant limitations and should be considered an initial screening tool for intelligence gathering instead of evidence collecting. The limitation of preserving only a cooperating witness or victim's inbox leaves a tremendous amount of valuable evidence uncollected. Fortunately, Facebook provides a system tool for recovering all available user information if the password to the account in known or can be recovered.

Using Facebook's DYI Download Tool

In cases where the victim is presenting evidence found on their Facebook profile, there is a way for the user to download their Facebook profile information. This is pursuant to a consent search of the victim's, or suspect's Facebook account. Facebook has created the Download Your Information (DYI) tool that allows a user to export all of the information they have posted, images, timelines, and other data collected by Facebook into a single portable document file (.PDF.)

To access this feature, the user must log in to both their Facebook page and the email account associated with the Facebook account. In the upper right corner of the Facebook page select the **down arrow** and then **Settings**.

Select **Download a copy of your Facebook data** below the General Account Settings.

Select **Start My Archive**

Select **Start My Archive** again because apparently the first time wasn't sufficient.

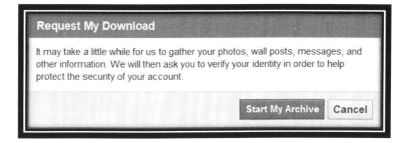

Select **Okay**.

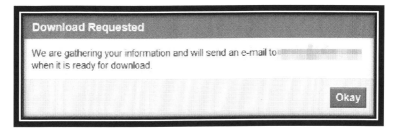

Facebook will create an archive containing all user generated and system generated information in a single, downloadable file. Once the archival process is complete the user will receive an email in the account associated with their Facebook profile. The user will then re-log into their Facebook account and be able to download the .PDF file.

Unfortunately, the DYI tool does not grab all of the information Facebook has regarding a user. Some of the items that are not included in the DYI consist for content sent to another user's account. For example, if User A posts a picture to the wall of User B, the posted picture would not be in the DYI download of User A unless it were still associated with their account. Similarly, 'tags', or other users' names to that picture are not available using the DYI tool. Some of the most important information available from Facebook is also not available using the DYI tool. This includes metadata associated with messages and media posts. The information the user sees in their DYI download is not the

61

same as the information available from Facebook with a legal de-mand. IP information is also unavailable to a user via the DYI tool.

There may be instances where parental consent or exigent cir-cumstances are sufficient to access this feature. However, the passwords for the Facebook account and the email account must be known.

Password Recovery Tools

There is also a method for using this feature against a suspect's Facebook account without their consent. This process should only be considered if the suspect has a Fourth Amendment waiver as a condition of probation or parole, exigent circumstances exist, or it is authorized via search warrant. Law enforcement officers should also be aware this process runs contrary to computer forensics principals, and may not be permissible under local laws and standard operating procedures. Check with the appropriate legal counsel before attempting this procedure.

To download the available information from a suspect's Facebook profile an investigator will need to have both their Facebook password and their email password. One method to obtain the user's Facebook password is to see if it is stored in the web browser used to access the account. Many people make use of the password storage feature found in web browsers such as Firefox, Internet Explorer, Chrome, and Safari.

When a user stores their passwords in their web browser they have an option to use a master password to protect the other stored passwords. Many people use the password storage feature of their web browsers but neglect to protect them with a master password. To detect any stored passwords it will be necessary to use a portable software program such as WebBrowserPassView from Nirsoft.net.

WebBrowserPassView is a free, portable application that can be installed on a USB drive and used to attempt to recover a suspect's stored passwords. Note that inserting a USB into a suspect's computer changes the underlying characteristics of the computer. This violates the core principal of computer forensics. Doing so also exposes the investigator's USB drive to any viruses or malware on the suspect's computer. Additionally, it raises the defense challenge that anything later discovered on the suspect's computer was placed there by the investigator or downloaded from the investigator's USB drive. Ideally, the processing of a live computer should be done by a computer forensic technician. However, there are situations and jurisdictions where a computer forensic examiner is not available to assist with the seizure of a live system. A careful balance needs to be stuck between the need to obtain the evidence immediately and the need to obtain the information in a forensically sound manner.

WebBrowserPassView can be downloaded for free from the site http://www.nirsoft.net/utils/web_browser_password.html.
Some anti-virus programs will detect the software as a virus or Trojan. This is a false alert. WebBrowserPassView is designed to search for and recover passwords from a system. This behavior is characteristic of a virus or Trojan but the program itself does not contain any infection. Recovered files are not transmitted anywhere and there is no risk to the investigator's or suspect's computers.

There is an alternative program if it is not possible to circumvent any virus detection software. Elcomsoft distributes a free password recovery tool called Facebook Password Extractor. It does the same thing as WebBrowserPassView.

Using WebBrowserPassView is simple. Download the program as a .ZIP file. This file will need to be unpacked to work. Law enforcement officers who do not have an unzipping program can download 7-Zip from http://www.7-zip.org/. 7-Zip is free and also portable so it does not need to be installed on an agency's computer.

Once the program is downloaded and unzipped transfer the files to a USB drive. To prevent a defense argument the suspect's computer was contaminated by evidence from other cases it is safest to use a new USB drive for this purpose.

Once WebBrowserPassView is installed on the USB drive it may be inserted into a target computer. Double click the Web-BrowserPassView icon and the program will immediately search for passwords stored in web browsers.

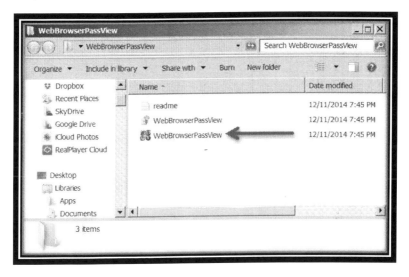

The usernames and passwords will be shown to on the right of the screen.

Obtaining the user's Facebook password is the first step in downloading their account information. Facebook will send an email link to the user's account to use the DYI download tool. This necessarily requires having the user's email password as well. Fortunately, there is a solution for this from NirSoft called MailPassView.

MailPassView is another free portable tool that recovers passwords from email clients such as:

- Outlook Express
- Microsoft Outlook 2002-2013
- Windows Mail
- Windows Live Mail
- IncrediMail
- Eudora
- Netscape 6.x/7.x (If the password is not encrypted with master password)
- Mozilla Thunderbird (If the password is not encrypted with master password)
- Group Mail Free
- Yahoo! Mail - If the password is saved in Yahoo! Messenger application.
- Hotmail/MSN mail - If the password is saved in MSN/Windows/Live Messenger application.

- Gmail - If the password is saved by Gmail Notifier application, Google Desktop, or by Google Talk.

Downloading and installing MailPassView is similar to using WebBrowserPassView. The software can be downloaded from http://www.nirsoft.net/utils/mailpv.html and unzipped onto a USB drive. Insert the USB into the target computer, run the program, and the software will recover the passwords from the listed email clients.

Once in possession of the Facebook password and the email client password the DYI tool can be used to recover all of the user's information.

Chapter 4: Understanding Your Legal Processes and Requirements

The technical solutions for obtaining information from a suspect's Facebook profile when it is private and/or the password is unknown are not especially pretty. In most cases, it will be necessary to serve the company with a legal demand for the information they retain. The only time Facebook will disclose information without a warrant is in the event of exigent circumstances, within the limits of your ongoing investigation. We will discuss this as well as delve into the process of serving Facebook legal demands for a range of law enforcement investigations.

Legal Considerations Concerning Private Accounts

Because Facebook also caters to users who create private accounts, there are some legal boundaries that you need to be aware of before you get started. It's important to identify where that line is before your get started. The following are some general guidelines you should adhere to while conducting an investigation:

- As a law enforcement officer, you can legally search any Facebook pages that are publically available, such as a public profile.
- Content such as pictures and messages and information from private profiles require a legal demand such as a search warrant, court order, or subpoena.

Considerations When Writing Legal Demands

Every legal demand will have its own specific language to a certain degree and writing one for Facebook won't be any different. It will be critical to use all of the correct nomenclature in your

68

descriptions. Recalling Chapter 1, we covered all of the specific Facebook data fields. Use and reference that list when writing you legal demands to ensure that they understand exactly what you are describing.

Equally important, is learning to ask only for data that is appropriate and relevant to the investigation. Obtaining 'everything' is usually unnecessary. Too much information could be perceived as overly broad or failing to meet the reasonable particularity requirement of a search warrant in a motion to suppress or appeal.

Many law enforcement officers use Facebook's language for the material they store. Specifically, "neoprint" and "photoprint." A neoprint is supposed to encapsulate all the user information and a photoprint is for all user images. However, not all of the information contained in the neoprint is necessarily related to every investigation. So, it may be necessary to tailor your language in a legal demand to obtain only what is relevant.

Exigent Circumstances

Facebook will only disclose account records in accordance with their Terms of Service (TOS) and applicable law. This means an investigator must have exigent circumstances to obtain the records or the appropriate legal process.

Facebook will disclose information without a search warrant, court order, or subpoena in the event of exigent circumstances. Exigent circumstances are defined as imminent threat to life or serious bodily injury. In most cases missing persons, abductions, child exploitation, suicidal subjects, and hostage situations are exigent circumstances. The closest analogy is if a law enforcement officer could enter a residence without a warrant in certain emergency situations, those same emergency situations can lead Facebook to divulge case specific information. Unfortunately, property crimes, pending vacations, and pressure from command staff do not count as exigent circumstances.

A common misperception involving exigent circumstances is that the officer's mere statement that a situation is exigent should suffice. This is not the case. The provider, in this case Facebook, must have a good faith belief there is an imminent threat to life or serious bodily injury. To satisfy the company's requirement it may be necessary to disclose certain facts and circumstances that lead the officer to come to that belief. If the company does not have grounds to believe an imminent threat to life exists, they may decline to provide information.

Exigent circumstances do not entitle an investigating officer to limitless data from Facebook. Only those items relevant and material to the ongoing investigation can be obtained. An investigator cannot request two years' worth of data using the exigent circumstances exception unless there are extenuating circumstances.

An important legal consideration in making exigent circumstances requests is the lack of judicial or legislative authority to do. Many law enforcement officers do not consider the legal ramifications of making an emergency request for information from Facebook or any other online or communications provider. The fact is, most states do not have a legal exception for obtaining information from a provider without legal process. While a provider may disclose information in an emergency to Federal law, the same disclosure can violate privacy provisions found in many state constitutions.

In the absence of a state law authorizing the release of information in an emergency without legal process it may be prudent to seek judicial authorization after the fact. Many providers inform law enforcement officers they have 48 hours after the release of information to provide them with legal process such as a search warrant, court order, or subpoena. The fact is there is no Federal requirement to do so. The only mention of obtaining judicial authorization after 48 hours is found in Federal statutes relating to exigent dialed number recorder/trap trace device installation, AKA pen registers, and exigent electronic surveillance or wiretaps.

Obtaining and serving legal process after the release of information pursuant to an exigent circumstances request, despite the lack of a legal mandate to do so, can protect an investigating law enforcement officer in two ways. First, the judicial authorization can shield the officer from civil liability for claims the suspect's rights to privacy under the state constitution were violated. Second, judicial authorization can protect other evidence that might be obtained as a result of the exigent circumstances request. For example, if a law enforcement officer obtains information from Facebook relating to a missing persons investigation but discovers additional evidence related to a child pornography case, they risk losing the evidence of other crimes. While the additional evidence may fall under the plain view doctrine, the discovery of information not relevant to the exigent circumstances case opens additional areas for challenge and litigation. Both of these pitfalls are mitigated by obtaining a search warrant, court order, or subpoena after the exigent circumstances request of information from Facebook.

Facebook staffs their Law Enforcement Response Team 24 hours a day, seven days a week. This is done through two centers, one if California and one in Dublin, Ireland. All emergency responses are done via the Law Enforcement Records Online (LEROS) system. There are no phone numbers to call or personal email addresses.

71

Navigating Facebook's Subpoena Compliance Department

Facebook's subpoena compliance department has a reputation for being difficult to deal with. There are no published phone numbers for anyone working in the department and officers who do have them guard them jealously. The 'hi-tech' people at Facebook refuse to accept facsimile copies because they view the technology as dated. Facebook appears to have zero regard for orders from judges to turn over records in a timely fashion. Facebook will not offer expert testimony in court.

Nothing will change unless and until a magistrate decides to hold Facebook accountable for impeding law enforcement investigations by finding them in contempt or issuing an order to show cause directing the company executives to appear and explain themselves.

For example, Facebook is located in California but is actually incorporated in Delaware. This makes them a foreign corporation doing business in California. Law enforcement officers in California are mostly unaware of California Penal Code Section 1524.2(b)(1) which states:

"When properly served with a search warrant issued by the California court, a foreign corporation subject to this section shall provide to the applicant, all records sought pursuant to that warrant within five business days of receipt, including those records maintained or located outside this state."

Facebook has five business days to respond to state search warrants issued by a California court. Unfortunately, many California law enforcement officers are unaware of this statute. Equally as unfortunate is the lack of judges willing to enforce this law.

Facebook Prioritizes Responses to Legal Action

In defense of Facebook, they do respond briskly to cases involving Internet Crimes Against Children task forces, child exploitation, suicide or homicide threats, and national security cases. However, 'routine' requests for cases involving gangs, narcotics, and organized crime are relegated to a lower priority. If the case under investigation involves imminent threat of serious bodily injury, loss of life, child exploitation, or national security issues the company must be notified of these circumstances when the legal process is submitted. Most law enforcement officers avoid sending the affidavit in support of the search warrant to Facebook for operational security reasons. Doing so prevents them from determining the priority of the legal demand and how it should be processed. If the case is important, but could be viewed mistakenly as 'routine' by their compliance department, make sure Facebook understands its significance.

Facebook will offer business records certification in accordance with Federal and State laws. However, they will not provide expert witness testimony in court about the information they collect, how it is collected, and how it is transmitted to investigating officers.

Out-of-State Legal Process

It is not uncommon for judges and magistrates in some states to believe they do not have jurisdiction over Facebook because the company is located in California and incorporated in Delaware. Their reasoning is often because they are a state judge in Michigan and, as the company is not located in their state, they do not have the authority to compel them to provide information under their state laws.

The strategy to combat a reluctant magistrate is to go to the website of the appropriate state agency responsible for licensing and regulating corporations. Every state has one. This may be the Secretary of State, the Office of the Comptroller, or, in this example, the Michigan Department of Licensing and Regulatory Affairs. Use a search engine and the keywords "STATE NAME + business entity search" or "STATE NAME + corporation search" to locate the appropriate state entity.

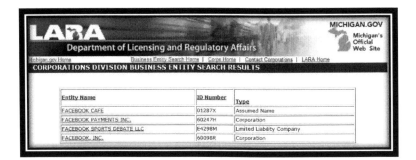

Once located, select Facebook, Inc. The results include the state entity name, identification number, and registered agent for service of process. This information helps establish the company is registered, and doing business in, the investigating officer's state. Therefore, the judge has jurisdiction and authority to order them to comply with a search warrant, court order, or subpoena.

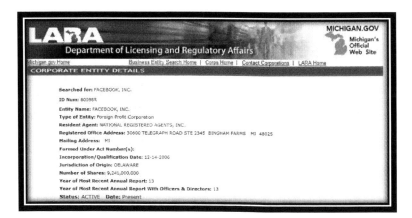

74

User Consent

Facebook will not accept consent to search forms signed by a user. All relevant information can be downloaded by the Facebook account holder using the steps previously outlined for the Download Your Information (DYI) process. The exception to available information using the DYI process is historical Internet Protocol information. Historical IP information can only be obtained via legal process; specifically, a search warrant.

Subpoena

A subpoena issues in connection with a criminal investigation will compel the disclosure of basic subscriber records. This includes username, length of service, credit card information, email address(es) and recent login/logout Internet Protocol (IP) addresses. A subpoena cannot be used to obtain anything that is considered content such as images, videos, chat messages, or email messages.

Court Order

A court order issues pursuant to Title 18 United States Code Section 2703(d) can compel the production of the same records as a subpoena with the inclusion of message headers and Internet Protocol (IP) addresses. A court order issued under this section cannot be used to obtain anything that is considered content such as images, videos, chat message, or email messages.

Search Warrant

A search warrant issued under the procedures described in the Federal Rules of Criminal Procedure or the equivalent state search warrant procedure can be used to compel the production of the stored content of any Facebook account. Stored content can include messages, images, videos, wall posts, and location information.

Search Warrant Example

The following Federal search warrant is an example from the Eastern District of California. It is a good template for the specific language for Facebook. The formatting and language should be adapted to the requirements of the jurisdiction for the investigating officer.

IN THE UNITED STATES DISTRICT COURT
FOR EASTERN DISTRICT OF CALIFORNIA

IN THE MATTER OF THE SEARCH OF INFORMATION ASSOCIATED WITH FACEBOOK USER ID [[**INSERT USER ID NUMBER**]] THAT IS STORED AT PREMISES OWNED, CONTROLLED, OR OPERATED BY FACEBOOK	Case No. _____ **Filed Under Seal**

AFFIDAVIT IN SUPPORT OF
AN APPLICATION FOR A SEARCH WARRANT

I, [[**AGENT NAME**]], being first duly sworn, hereby depose and state as follows:

INTRODUCTION AND AGENT BACKGROUND

1.   I make this affidavit in support of an application for a search warrant for information associated with certain Facebook accounts that is stored at premises owned, maintained, controlled, or operated by Facebook, a social networking company headquartered in Palo Alto, California. The information to be searched is described in the following

paragraphs and in Attachment A. This affidavit is made in support of an application for a search warrant under 18 U.S.C. §§ 2703(a), 2703(b)(1)(A) and 2703(c)(1)(A) to require Facebook to disclose to the government records and other information in its possession, pertaining to the subscriber or customer operating the web sites.

2. I am a Special Agent with the [[**AGENCY**]], and have been since [[**DATE**]]. [[**DESCRIBE TRAINING AND EXPERIENCE TO THE EXTENT IT SHOWS QUALIFICATION TO SPEAK ABOUT THE INTERNET AND OTHER TECHNICAL MATTERS**]].

3. The facts in this affidavit come from my personal observations, my training and experience, and information obtained from other agents and witnesses. This affidavit is intended to show merely that there is sufficient probable cause for the requested warrant and does not set forth all of my knowledge about this matter.

4. Based on my training and experience and the facts as set forth in this affidavit, there is probable cause to believe that violations of [[**STATUTES**]] have been committed by [[**SUSPECTS** or unknown persons]]. There is also probable cause to search the information described in Attachment A for evidence of these crimes [[and contraband or fruits of these crimes]], as described in Attachment B.

PROBABLE CAUSE

5. [[**Give facts establishing probable cause. At a minimum, establish a connection between the Facebook account and a suspected crime; mention whether a preservation request was sent (or other facts suggesting Facebook still has the records desired)**]]

6. Facebook owns and operates a free-access social networking website of the same name that can be accessed at

77

http://www.facebook.com. Facebook allows its users to establish accounts with Facebook, and users can then use their accounts to share written news, photographs, videos, and other information with other Facebook users, and sometimes with the general public.

7.　　Facebook asks users to provide basic contact information to Facebook, either during the registration process or thereafter. This information may include the user's full name, birth date, contact e-mail addresses, physical address (including city, state, and zip code), telephone numbers, screen names, websites, and other personal identifiers. Facebook also assigns a user identification number to each account.

8.　　Facebook users can select different levels of privacy for the communications and information associated with their Facebook accounts. By adjusting these privacy settings, a Facebook user can make information available only to himself or herself, to particular Facebook users, to all Facebook users, or to anyone with access to the Internet, including people who are not Facebook users. Facebook accounts also include other account settings that users can adjust to control, for example, the types of notifications they receive from Facebook.

9.　　Facebook users may join one or more groups or networks to connect and interact with other users who are members of the same group or network. A Facebook user can also connect directly with individual Facebook users by sending each user a "Friend Request." If the recipient of a "Friend Request" accepts the request, then the two users will become "Friends" for purposes of Facebook and can exchange communications or view information about each other. Each Facebook user's account includes a list of that user's "Friends" and a "Mini-Feed," which highlights information about the user's "Friends," such as profile changes, upcoming events, and birthdays.

10.   Facebook users can create profiles that include photographs, lists of personal interests, and other information. Facebook users can also post "status" updates about their whereabouts and actions, as well as links to videos, photographs, articles, and other items available elsewhere on the Internet. Facebook users can also post information about upcoming "events," such as social occasions, by listing the event's time, location, host, and guest list. A particular user's profile page also includes a "Wall," which is a space where the user and his or her "Friends" can post messages, attachments, and links that will typically be visible to anyone who can view the user's profile.

11.   Facebook has a Photos application, where users can upload an unlimited number of albums and photos. Another feature of the Photos application is the ability to "tag" (i.e., label) other Facebook users in a photo or video. When a user is tagged in a photo or video, he or she receives a notification of the tag and a link to see the photo or video. For Facebook's purposes, a user's "Photoprint" includes all photos uploaded by that user that have not been deleted, as well as all photos uploaded by any user that have that user tagged in them.

12.   Facebook users can exchange private messages on Facebook with other users. These messages, which are similar to e-mail messages, are sent to the recipient's "Inbox" on Facebook, which also stores copies of messages sent by the recipient, as well as other information. Facebook users can also post comments on the Facebook profiles of other users or on their own profiles; such comments are typically associated with a specific posting or item on the profile.

13.   Facebook Notes is a blogging feature available to Facebook users, and it enables users to write and post notes or personal web logs ("blogs"), or to import their blogs from other services, such as Xanga, LiveJournal, and Blogger.

14.   The Facebook Gifts feature allows users to send virtual "gifts" to their friends that appear as icons on the recipient's profile page. Gifts cost money to purchase, and a personalized message can be attached to each gift. Facebook users can also send each other "pokes," which are free and simply result in a notification to the recipient that he or she has been "poked" by the sender.

15.   Facebook also has a Marketplace feature, which allows users to post free classified ads. Users can post items for sale, housing, jobs, and other items on the Marketplace.

16.   In addition to the applications described above, Facebook also provides its users with access to thousands of other applications on the Facebook platform. When a Facebook user accesses or uses one of these applications, an update about that the user's access or use of that application may appear on the user's profile page.

17.   [[**For requests for information about a Facebook group:** Some Facebook pages are affiliated with groups of users, rather than one individual user. Membership in the group is monitored and regulated by the administrator or head of the group, who can invite new members and reject or accept requests by users to enter. Facebook can identify all users who are currently registered to a particular group and can identify the administrator and/or creator of the group. Facebook also assigns a group identification number to each group. Facebook uses the term "Group Contact Info" to describe the contact information for the group's creator and/or administrator, as well as a PDF of the current status of the group profile page.]]

18.   Facebook uses the term "Neoprint" to describe an expanded view of a given user profile. The "Neoprint" for a given user can include the following information from the user's profile: profile contact information; Mini-Feed information;

status updates; links to videos, photographs, articles, and other items; Notes; Wall postings; friend lists, including the friends' Facebook user identification numbers; groups and networks of which the user is a member, including the groups' Facebook group identification numbers; future and past event postings; rejected "Friend" requests; comments; gifts; pokes; tags; and information about the user's access and use of Facebook applications.

19.   Facebook also retains Internet Protocol ("IP") logs for a given user ID or IP address. These logs may contain information about the actions taken by the user ID or IP address on Facebook, including information about the type of action, the date and time of the action, and the user ID and IP address associated with the action. For example, if a user views a Facebook profile, that user's IP log would reflect the fact that the user viewed the profile, and would show when and from what IP address the user did so.

20.   Social networking providers like Facebook typically retain additional information about their users' accounts, such as information about the length of service (including start date), the types of service utilized, and the means and source of any payments associated with the service (including any credit card or bank account number). In some cases, Facebook users may communicate directly with Facebook about issues relating to their account, such as technical problems, billing inquiries, or complaints from other users. Social networking providers like Facebook typically retain records about such communications, including records of contacts between the user and the provider's support services, as well records of any actions taken by the provider or user as a result of the communications.

21.   Therefore, the computers of Facebook are likely to contain all the material just described, including stored electronic communications and information concerning

subscribers and their use of Facebook, such as account access information, transaction information, and account application.

INFORMATION TO BE SEARCHED AND THINGS TO BE SEIZED

22.   I anticipate executing this warrant under the Electronic Communications Privacy Act, in particular 18 U.S.C. §§ 2703(a), 2703(b)(1)(A) and 2703(c)(1)(A), by using the warrant to require Facebook to disclose to the government copies of the records and other information (including the content of communications) particularly described in Section I of Attachment B. Upon receipt of the information described in Section I of Attachment B, government-authorized persons will review that information to locate the items described in Section II of Attachment B.

CONCLUSION

23.   Based on the forgoing, I request that the Court issue the proposed search warrant.

24.   This Court has jurisdiction to issue the requested warrant because it is "a court of competent jurisdiction" as defined by 18 U.S.C. § 2711. 18 U.S.C. §§ 2703(a), (b)(1)(A) & (c)(1)(A). Specifically, the Court **[[CHOOSE ONE OR MORE:** [is "a district court of the United States . . . that – has jurisdiction over the offense being investigated." 18 U.S.C. § 2711(3)(A)(i).] **AND/OR** ["is in . . . a district in which the provider . . . is located or in which the wire or electronic communications, records, or other information are stored." 18 U.S.C. § 2711(3)(A)(ii).] **AND/OR** ["is acting on a request for foreign assistance pursuant to [18 U.S.C. § 3512]." 18 U.S.C. § 2711(3)(A)(iii).]]

25.   Pursuant to 18 U.S.C. § 2703(g), the presence of a law enforcement officer is not required for the service or execution of this warrant.

REQUEST FOR SEALING

26.   [[**If you want to file under seal, you can insert this language in the affidavit:** I further request that the Court order that all papers in support of this application, including the affidavit and search warrant, be sealed until further order of the Court. These documents discuss an ongoing criminal investigation that is neither public nor known to all of the targets of the investigation. Accordingly, there is good cause to seal these documents because their premature disclosure may seriously jeopardize that investigation.]]

Respectfully submitted,

_____

[[**AGENT NAME**[]
Special Agent
[[**AGENCY**]]

Subscribed and sworn to before me on
_____, 201___

_____

UNITED STATES MAGISTRATE JUDGE

ATTACHMENT A

Property to Be Searched

This warrant applies to information associated with the Facebook user ID [[**IDENTIFY USER ID NUMBER**]] that is stored at premises owned, maintained, controlled, or operated by Facebook, a company headquartered in Palo Alto, California.

ATTACHMENT B

Particular Things to be Seized
I.   Information to be disclosed by Facebook

To the extent that the information described in Attachment A is within the possession, custody, or control of Facebook, including any messages, records, files, logs, or information that have been deleted but are still available to Facebook, or have been preserved pursuant to a request made under 18 U.S.C. § 2703(f), Facebook is required to disclose the following information to the government for each user ID listed in Attachment A:

(a)   All contact information, including **[[for user IDs:** full name, user identification number, birth date, contact e-mail addresses, physical address (including city, state, and zip code), telephone numbers, screen names, websites, and other personal identifiers.]] [[**for group IDs:** group identification number, a list of users currently registered to the group, and Group Contact Info, including all contact information for the creator and/or administrator of the group and a PDF of the current status of the group profile page.]]

(b)   All Photoprints, including all photos uploaded by that user ID and all photos uploaded by any user that have that user tagged in them;

(c)   All Neoprints, including profile contact information; News Feed information; status updates; links to videos, photographs, articles, and other Items; Notes; Wall postings; friend lists, including the friends' Facebook user identification numbers; groups and networks of which the user is a member, including the groups' Facebook group identification numbers;

future and past event postings; rejected "Friend" requests; comments; gifts; pokes; tags; and information about the user's access and use of Facebook applications;

(d)   All activity logs for the account and all other documents showing the user's posts and other Facebook activities;

(e)   All other records of communications and messages made or received by the user, including all private messages, chat history, video calling history, and pending "Friend" requests;

(f)   All "check ins" and other location information;

(g)   All IP logs, including all records of the IP addresses that logged into the account;

(h)   All records of the account's usage of the "Like" feature, including all Facebook posts and all non-Facebook webpages and content that the user has "liked";

(i)   All information about the Facebook pages that the account is or was a "fan" of;

(j)   All past and present lists of friends created by the account;

(k)   All records of Facebook searches performed by the account;

(l)   All information about the user's access and use of Facebook Marketplace;

86

(m)   The length of service (including start date), the types of service utilized by the user, and the means and source of any payments associated with the service (including any credit card or bank account number);

(n)   All privacy settings and other account settings, including privacy settings for individual Facebook posts and activities, and all records showing which Facebook users have been blocked by the account;

(o)   All records pertaining to communications between Facebook and any person regarding the user or the user's Facebook account, including contacts with support services and records of actions taken.

II.   Information to be seized by the government

All information described above in Section I that constitutes fruits, evidence and instrumentalities of violations of [[**STATUTES**]] involving [[**SUSPECT**]] since [[**DATE**]], including, for each user ID identified on Attachment A, information pertaining to the following matters:

(a) [[**insert specific descriptions of the records which your probable cause supports seizure and copying of; example: "Messages, correspondence, documents and records pertaining to …**

"the sale of illegal drugs," "a threat to bomb a laboratory," … communications between John and Mary," "robberies or other violent crimes," the possession, ownership, or use of any firearms," "the location of the account user," "preparatory steps taken in furtherance of the

scheme." Tailor the list to items that would be helpful to the investigation.]]

(b) Records relating to who created, used, or communicated with the user ID, including records about their identities and whereabouts.

CERTIFICATE OF AUTHENTICITY OF DOMESTIC BUSINESS
RECORDS PURSUANT TO FEDERAL RULE OF EVIDENCE 902(11)

I, _____, attest, under penalties of perjury under the laws of the United States of America pursuant to 28 U.S.C. § 1746, that the information contained in this declaration is true and correct. I am employed by Facebook, and my official title is

_____. I am a custodian of records for Facebook. I state that each of the records attached hereto is the original record or a true duplicate of the original record in the custody of Facebook, and that I am the custodian of the attached records consisting of _____ (pages/CDs/kilobytes). I further state that:

a.   all records attached to this certificate were made at or near the time of the occurrence of the matter set forth, by, or from information transmitted by, a person with knowledge of those matters;

b.   such records were kept in the ordinary course of a regularly conducted business activity of Facebook; and

c.   such records were made by Facebook as a regular practice.

I further state that this certification is intended to satisfy Rule 902(11) of the Federal Rules of Evidence.

_____   _____

Date   Signature

Non-Disclosure Orders

After Edward Snowden betrayed his country by stealing and releasing classified documents, the high-tech community has bent over backwards to avoid the appearance of cooperating with the government. One of the reactions adopted by many social media and Internet companies, including Facebook, has been a practice of going out of their way to notify their customers when they receive a legal demand from law enforcement. Unless specifically ordered not to do so Facebook will notify a criminal suspect of the receipt of a search warrant, court order, or subpoena for their information.

Facebook has an internal policy whereby they will notify their customers of the receipt of legal process within seven days unless expressly prohibited from doing so. During that time, Facebook states they will **attempt** to notify the submitting law enforcement officer during prior to the eighth day. The submitting officer has several options including retracting the legal demand or obtaining a sealing order.

To prevent the suspect from being notified about the existence of a search warrant, court order, or subpoena Facebook must be ordered by a magistrate not to do so. Many law enforcement officers are used to sealing their search warrants. Unfortunately, sealing the warrant affidavit is insufficient to prevent Facebook from disclosing receipt of the warrant. Specific non-disclosure language must be included in the originally submitted search warrant directing Facebook not to disclose the existence of the warrant.

Investigators who have already submitted a legal demand to Facebook have two options. Retract the search warrant and obtain a new one with the nondisclosure statement or obtain a separate sealing order after the fact.

Nondisclosure language in a search warrant may specify the length of time Facebook is prevented from disclosing the warrant. These may be in increments of time such as 30, 60, or 90 days. Law enforcement officers should be cautious about using a finite number of days or a specific date for when the company can notify their customer. It is not uncommon for a 'simple' investigation to become complex after the investigation of one Facebook account. This is particularly true for investigations involving child pornography, child exploitation, human trafficking, gangs, and narcotics. As the investigation progresses the clock on the original legal demand is ticking. Facebook may notify the original suspect just as the larger investigation comes to fruition. This may seriously impair the investigation into the underlying conspiracy.

An alternate strategy for nondisclosure language is to request the authorizing judge prevent Facebook from disclosing the existence of the search warrant until further order of the court. Facebook would be prevented from notifying their customer until the original law enforcement officer sought an additional court order authorizing the company to notify them, the suspect's legal representation sought an order from the court authorizing their client to be notified, or the company sought a court order authorizing the notification. None of those situations are likely so the effect of the nondisclosure order would be to prevent notification for the duration of the investigation.

Some magistrates object to preventing notification indefinitely. An alternate strategy would be to request Facebook be prevented from disclosing the receipt of the legal demand until the suspect has been arrested for the crime under investigation. This may be a more palatable strategy as Federal search warrants and grand jury indictments remain sealed until they are executed or the suspect is arrested for the charge.

Simply requesting non-disclosure by Facebook is insufficient. The reason for non-disclosure must be supported in the search warrant affidavit. Guidance for the justification of a nondisclosure order can be found in 18 USC § 2705(b). While this section only applies to non-disclosure for court order obtained pursuant to 18 USC § 2705(b) the language can be adopted and utilized for state search warrants.

Ground for nondisclosure may include:

- Endangering the life or physical safety of an individual

Your Affiant is aware Facebook has a policy of notifying their customers seven days after receipt of process such as a search warrant. Your Affiant believes notification to the suspect of receipt of this Search Warrant by Facebook would cause them to become aware of the law enforcement investigation. Your Affiant believes, upon being notified of the law enforcement investigation the suspects, known and unknown, would take steps to accelerate their plans to commit homicide or serious bodily injury against their intended victim. Therefore, your Affiant requests Facebook be prevented from disclosing the existence of the Search Warrant to the suspect or any other person not directly involved with complying seeks until further order of the Court.

- Flight from prosecution

Your Affiant is aware Facebook has a policy of notifying their customers seven days after receipt of process such as a search warrant. Your Affiant believes notification to the suspect of receipt of this Search Warrant by Facebook would cause them to become aware of the law enforcement investigation. Your Affiant believes, upon being notified of the law enforcement investigation the suspect would immediately flee the jurisdiction of this court. Thus far the investigation has revealed the suspect has multiple family members in Mexico and frequent contact with those family members via cellular telephone and electronic mail. Your Affiant believes if the suspect were aware of the investigation they would seek refuge from those same family members. Therefore, your Affiant requests Facebook be prevented from disclosing the existence of the Search Warrant to the suspect or any other person not directly involved with complying seeks until further order of the Court.

- Destruction of or tampering with evidence

Your Affiant is aware Facebook has a policy of notifying their customers seven days after receipt of process such as a search warrant. Your Affiant believes notification to the suspect of receipt of this Search Warrant by Facebook would cause them to become aware of the law enforcement investigation. Your Affiant believes, upon being notified of the law enforcement investigation they would conceal, secrete, delete, destroy or encrypt the very evidence this Affidavit for Search Warrant seeks to retrieve and preserve. Through the investigation your Affiant has become aware the suspect has sufficient technical proficiency to seriously impede or prevent subsequent forensic examination of their computer, mobile devices, and removable storage media using secure deletion methods, software encryption, and/or physical destruction of the devices. Therefore, your Affiant requests Facebook be prevented from disclosing the existence of the Search Warrant to the suspect or any other person not directly involved with complying seeks until further order of the Court.

- Intimidation of potential witnesses

Your Affiant is aware Facebook has a policy of notifying their customers seven days after receipt of process such as a search warrant. Your Affiant believes notification to the suspect of receipt of this Search Warrant by Facebook would cause them to become aware of the law enforcement investigation. Your Affiant believes, upon being notified of the law enforcement investigation they would seek to intimidate witnesses and/or the victim in this investigation. Your Affiant is aware the suspect is a validated member of the West Side Locos (WSL) street gang. Your Affiant is further aware WSL gang members have a documented history of threatening victims and witnesses to prevent them from cooperating with law enforcement investigations and/or testifying in court. Your Affiant is further aware WSL gang members have a documented history in retaliating against victims and witnesses who do cooperate with law enforcement investigations and/or testify in court. Therefore, your Affiant requests Facebook be prevented from disclosing the existence of the Search Warrant to the suspect or any other person not directly involved with complying seeks until further order of the Court.

- Otherwise seriously jeopardizing an investigation or unduly delaying a trial

Your Affiant is aware Facebook has a policy of notifying their customers seven days after receipt of process such as a search warrant. Your Affiant believes notification to the suspect of receipt of this Search Warrant by Facebook would cause them to become aware of the law enforcement investigation. Your Affiant believes, upon being notified of the law enforcement investigation they would conceal, secrete, delete, destroy or encrypt the very evidence this Affidavit for Search Warrant seeks to retrieve and preserve. Your Affiant also believes the suspect may attempt to dissuade witnesses from cooperating with the law enforcement investigation and/or testifying in court. Notification would also allow the suspect to conspire with others to create alibis and fabricate a version of events to avoid successful prosecution. Therefore, your Affiant requests Facebook be prevented from disclosing the existence of the Search Warrant to the suspect or any other person not directly involved with complying seeks until further order of the Court.

94

Chapter 5: Developing Investigative Leads from Facebook

Phone Numbers Provided by Facebook

One of the investigative leads provided from Facebook are phone numbers. Facebook users have verified phone numbers added to their accounts for security verification purposes. These phone numbers do not usually show up in the user profile but they are stored by the company. Associated phone numbers are listed in the order they were added to the account with the oldest being at the bottom and the most recent at the top. The date the phone number was verified is also maintained by Facebook.

One of the major challenges with investigating mobile phone numbers is figuring out who the provider is and how to contact them. To address the first issue many law enforcement investigators rely on free or commercial websites such as Google, Accurint, CLEAR, TLO, and LPPolice. These online services should be considered as a pointer system but there is no guarantee of reliability.

One of the most commonly used free tools to determine the provider to a phone number is fonefinder.net. While this site is an option for general phone number lookup information it suffers from a fatal flaw-notably the proprietor's inability to track number portability.

CORE SKILL: Investigating Phone Numbers

Number Portability

Number Portability refers to the ability to change, or port, a phone number from one provider to another. In the bad old days if you wanted to change providers, for example from AT&T to Sprint, you had to obtain an entirely new phone number. This is no longer the case and a consumer can change their providers while keeping the phone number that was originally assigned to them by the original carrier. User of free websites like fonefinder.net usually fail to read the FAQ section which states:

> Bottom Line: FoneFinder is inaccurate to the extent that numbers have been ported.

This creates a problem for law enforcement investigators. Submitting a search warrant, court order, or subpoena to the wrong provider can cause unnecessary delay in receiving the results and consequently delay or stall the investigation.

For example, examine the following results for the phone number 510-750-####. Fonefinder.com reveals the number is assigned to Nextel Communications. This should be an immediate red-flag to many law enforcement officers as it is common knowledge Nextel Communications was acquired by Sprint in 2005 and stopped providing push to talk service in June 2013. In fact, this number has been ported to Verizon. Investigators who serve Sprint with a legal demand can expect to have their investigation delayed until the subpoena compliance department figures out the phone number is not serviced by their network.

Area Code	Prefix	City/Switch Name (Click for city search)	State/Prov. Area Map	Telephone Company Web link	Telco Type	Map/Zip Detail
510	750	HAYWARD	California	NEXTEL COMMUNICATIONS, INC.	WIRELESS PROV	CALIFORNIA The Golden State

A Free Resource to Check Number Portability

Free online and commercial services can be a place to start. However, an investigator will need to verify who the provider is prior to submitting legal demands. The best way to do this is to check the phone number in the Number Portability Administration Center's (NPAC) Interactive Voice Response (IVR) system. NPAC is an industry neutral group and is responsible for coordinating the transfer of ported phone numbers from one provider to another. During the transfer process, NPAC tracks the destination of the ported number and makes the information available to law enforcement through the IVR system.

To access the IVR system, law enforcement officers should go to the NPAC website and register for access from their website at http://www.npac.com/the-npac/access/law-enforcement-agencies-psaps/ivr-system.

The IVR System

To use the IVR System, U.S. Law Enforcement Agencies, Public Safety Providers and 911 Service Providers must first register via the IVR Registration Form and receive a Personal Identification Number (PIN). Follow the IVR Process Flow Instructions (provided below) to retrieve data on up to 20 telephone numbers per call.

Use of the IVR System, including requesting or receiving a PIN, is strictly limited to:

- **Law Enforcement Agencies**: agencies in the United States or of a State or political subdivision thereof that are empowered by law to conduct investigations of or to make arrests for violations of federal, state or local laws; and
- **Public Safety Answering Point Providers**: entities in the U.S. that perform Public Safety Answering Point (PSAP) functions in the performance of their official duties.

PINs can be shared within an organization. If your organization has already been assigned a PIN, please use that PIN. If your organization has not been assigned a PIN, please submit only one registration form to request a PIN for your organization's use. If each individual in your organization requires a unique PIN assignment, please submit a separate registration form for each individual.

Request IVR PIN

For additional assistance, contact IVR Support:
Phone: 571-434-5432
Email: IVR@Neustar.biz

For questions regarding the receipt of your PIN, contact:
Peggy Gilliam
Phone: 502-653-3860
Email: peggy.gilliam@Neustar.biz

Clicking on the Request IVR PIN button will take the user to the registration page. Submit the form with your official contact information and wait for them to respond. Once approved, you will be contacted via phone with a PIN number assigned to your agency.

Once access has been granted users can call in to the IVR access numbers 571-434-5781 or, if this number is unavailable, users may call 704-583-8311 to reach the Secondary IVR system. After calling in users will provide the agency PIN and the target phone number. An automated response will notify you if the number has been ported, and if so, who the current provider is.

The sad truth is that many law enforcement agencies have already registered for the IVR service and have been issued a PIN. As the PIN is specific to an agency it is incumbent upon the person registering the agency to share the number with their fellow law enforcement officers. Sometimes, this doesn't happen as many agencies have discovered this when they register only to find out someone in their department has already done so and been issued the PIN. The PIN number is assigned to the agency and should be shared with everyone who has a need, or may have a need for it. The PIN number should not be hoarded by an individual or unit within the larger organization.

Once the provider has been determined, the second challenge arises which is determining the point of contact to serve with the legal demand.

Using Search.org to Identify Cell Phone Service Providers

Many law enforcement investigators use a free service provided by The National Consortium for Justice Information and Statistics, commonly known by their website address as search.org. The website offers a number of resources to law enforcement in a variety of disciplines but it is most commonly used for the ISP (Internet Service Provider) List feature. The ISP List originated as a way for law enforcement investigators to share contact information for Internet-based companies. However, the contents of the ISP List have expanded to include other companies such as cell phone service providers and landline carriers. For this reason, it is the first stop for many law enforcement investigators seeking to locate the proper point of contact for service of process.

To access the Internet Service Provider (ISP) list, go to http://www.search.org/resources/isp-list/. This will bring up an alphabetized drop down list and you can scroll down for your provider.

Various, Inc.
Veeay.com
VeriSign Worldwide Headquarters
Verizon FiOS
Verizon Internet Services
Verizon Landlines (North Central)
Verizon Online
Verizon Online in Vermont, Maine and New Hampshire
Verizon Wireless Legal Compliance
Vermont Telephone Company (VTEL)
VFEmail
VideoBam
Virgin Mobile USA
VISA
Visionary Communications, Inc.
Vodhelp.com
Volcano Internet
Volonet Technologies
Vonage
VPLS.net

The results are reliant upon the information provided by submitting law enforcement officers. In the example below you can see that in addition to the contact information for serving AT&T the submitter included warning notes about difficulties in obtaining information during an exigent circumstances case. Other notes include their refusal to provide historical cell site location information without a search warrant or court order. This information is important and can help an investigator receive their data back in a timely manner so pay attention to the notes.

101

AT&T Wireless

Online Service: AT&T Wireless

Online Service Address: 208 South Akard, 10th Floor
Dallas, Texas 75202
USA

Phone Number: 800-291-4952

Fax Number: 248-552-3201

Note(s): AT&T says they cannot accept any service by email.

For Subpoena's Address:
3 ATT Plaza
308 South Akard Street – 14th Floor – M
Dallas, TX 75202

Phone: 800-291-4952
Fax: 248-552-3201

For Search Warrants and Court Order fax: 888-938-4715.

Please note:
*** AT&T WILL charge $40 per hour to process a subpoena, and they do not notify you first.
*** AT&T took 9 days to respond to a subpoena, even marked EMERGENCY MATTER – MISSING ENDANGERED CHILD.
*** AT&T WILL NOT provide cell site / tower location / phone location without a Search Warrant or Court Order – regardless of the case being a missing endangered child.

It is also important to check the Last Updated field. Some of the companies listed on the ISP List are defunct. In other cases the data is old and has not been updated.

This service from SEARCH relies on input from law enforcement officers who submit their information for inclusion in the ISP List menu. It is only as good as the information put into it and I encourage users who have the subpoena compliance contact information for small or regional carriers to submit the information. This is especially valuable if you have ever struggled to find a point of contact at a small or esoteric service. Consider your fellow law enforcement investigators and share the information.

The ISP List feature works well for large, well-known cellular service providers and many smaller regional providers. But it is not an all-inclusive list.

Leveraging IP Addresses Provided by Facebook

Whether you are a patrol officer in a small agency or a Detective at a large department, if you are going to investigate Facebook, you must understand IP addresses and how to examine them.

Every device involved in communicating on the Internet uses an IP address. IP addresses come in two versions IPv4 and IPv6. IPv4 addresses consist of 4 numbers ranging from 0 to 255, separated by periods.

```
110.311.148.31
```

The total number of variations of IPv4 addresses is roughly 4.3 billion. With the explosion of the Internet, personal computers, laptops, tablets, cell phones, and wearable technology the number of IPv4 addresses is insufficient to meet the anticipated demand. IPv6 addresses were developed to increase the pool of available numbers. IPv6 addresses have eight groups of four alphanumeric characters separated by colons. An example of a full IPv6 address is:

```
FE80:0000:0000:0000:0202:B3FF:FE1E:8329
```

An IPv6 address may be collapses to shorten the total number of characters. An example of a collapsed IPv6 addresses is:

```
FE80::0202:B3FF:FE1E:8329
```

The consecutive colons (::) notation is used to represent four successive blocks that contain all zeros.

Computers and other devices may be assigned an IPv4 or IPv6 Internet protocol address by an Internet service provider. An Internet service provider (ISP) is usually a commercial vendor providing service but may also be a business or government organization. They may reserve or be assigned block of IPv4 addresses that are assigned to their users. An IPv4 address can roughly be compared to a phone number assigned to a particular device. Unfortunately, it can get complicated as there are three types of IPv4 addresses:

Static-IP addresses are permanently assigned to devices. An entity, such as Facebook, maintaining a constant presence on the Internet usually requires a static IP address.

Dynamic-IP addresses are temporarily assigned from a pool of available addresses registered to an ISP. These addresses area assigned to a computer or mobile device when as user begins an online session. A dynamic IP address may vary from one logon session to the next.

Semi-Dynamic-These IP addresses are technically dynamic but may be assigned to a particular device for a prolonged period of time.

CORE SKILL: Tracing IP Addresses

Some of the most valuable information that comes from Facebook, and communications that occur outside of Facebook, are the IP addresses. An investigator can use the IP address the determine where the suspect is accessing Facebook from or the Internet Service Provider and location of an email message sent outside of Facebook .

There are many free website to trace an IP address. For way of illustration, the following images are from whatismyipaddress.com. The information from each publicly available website is identical so it often a matter of user preference for an interface.

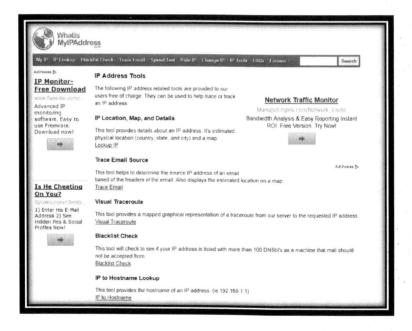

To trace an IP address, first copy the originating IP address from the email you are interested in. Next go to whichever website you are going to use to trace the IP address. In this case, from the whatismyipaddress.com website, click on the blue link that says Lookup IP.

IP Location, Map, and Details

This tool provides details about an IP address. It's estimated physical location (country, state, and city) and a map.
Lookup IP

Clicking the link will bring up the screen below.

Lookup IP Address Location

These details include the hostname, Geographic location information (includes country, region/state, city, latitude, longitude and telephone area code.), and a location specific map.

Geolocation technology can never be 100% accurate in providing the location of an IP address. When the IP address is a proxy server and it does not expose the user's IP address it is virtually impossible to locate the user. The country accuracy is estimated at about 99%. For IP addresses in the United States, it is 90% accurate on the state level, and 81% accurate within a 25 mile radius. Our world-wide users indicate 55% accurate within 25km.

Please enter the IP address you want to lookup below:

70.199.87.91   Lookup IP Address

The website will automatically bring up the public information about the IP address. You will see a lot of information is available including the ISP provider (Verizon Wireless) and the general geographic location (Tracy, CA).

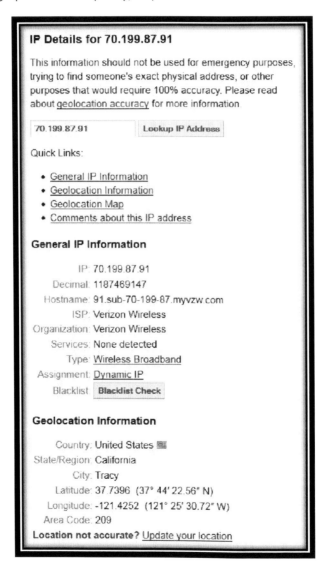

108

The results of tracing the IP address will reveal the Internet Service Provider (ISP), the organization name if the IP address is assigned to a business or government organization, whether the IP address is dynamic or static, and some general location data.

Working With Gmail IP Addresses

It is not uncommon for communications that started on Facebook to end up with emails outside of the social media service. Google's Gmail is one of the largest and most popular email services but it presents a unique problem. The Gmail service sometimes omits the sender IP address information from the message header. If the email was sent from a Gmail account within a web browser only the IP address of Gmail's mail server is shown in **Received: from**. However, if the message is sent from a different email client, or a mobile device, the IP address will still be there. To see if an email message has header information, select the desired email and then click the drop down arrow in the right corner of the inbox. Select **Show original** and a new tab will open showing the message header information.

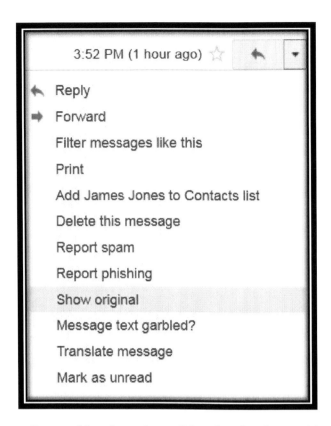

If manually searching through email headers for the IP address of an email message is overly complex, there is a free tool from Google to help decipher the path an email took. You will still need to locate the header information in the email. But instead of searching and trying to locate the originating IP address the information can be quickly deciphered using the website https://toolbox.googleapps.com/apps/messageheader/. This tool will show you some basic information about the header of the message but does not return the same information as websites such as whatismyipaddress.com

To resolve an IP address back to a specific device, the date and time the IP address was assigned must be determined. Further complicating the investigation of IPv4 addresses is some mobile providers have a finite pool of these addresses. It is not uncommon the find a cellular service provider only has four to ten IPv4 addresses for all of their subscribers. Determining a suspect device in this situation can be impossible.

The introduction of IPv6 means that every device will have a unique IP address. However, the transition from IPv4 to IPv6 has not been fully implemented and will not be for several years.

The ISP can determine which of their customers was assigned the IP address. They require the IP address, the date, the time, and the time zone used to record the time. An ISP will not release this data without a legal demand such as a search warrant, court order, or subpoena. For residential Internet customers, the ISP will be able to return the customer information including subscriber data such as name, address, phone number, and billing information. This data can be very important in Facebook investigations.

To determine whom to serve with a legal demand, first determine the ISP. To find their address for service of process many investigators use the lookup tool found at the website http://www.search.org/resources/isp-list/

Find the appropriate provider from the main drop down menu.

The same website can be used to find the legal compliance of-fices for most major email providers.

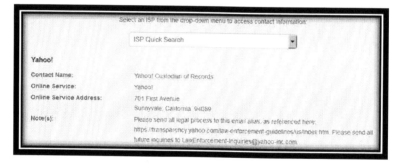

Using Images, Videos, and Documents from Facebook

Images are some of the most sought after evidence and intelligence from Facebook. Images and videos posted to a criminal suspect's Facebook account can give investigators valuable clue in many different types of investigations. Additionally, there is information encoded within the image files themselves that can reveal the date and time the image was taken, the type of camera or mobile device used to take the image, and, in some cases, the global positioning system coordinates where the pictures was taken.

Detecting and Examining EXIF Data

Metadata, sometimes referred to as EXIF data is often defined as data about data. More properly it is data about the container or properties of a file. EXIF stands for Exchangeable Image File Format and a common standard for formatting images and sounds. It is also used for information in images from digital cameras, including mobile devices. EXIF data consists of numerous attributes about a digital image including, the orientation of the device, focal length, flash settings, and ISO speeds. Most investigators are concerned with the make and model of the device used to take the image, the date the image was taken, and, when enabled, the global positioning system (GPS) coordinates where the image was taken.

It is important to remember that EXIF data can be changed by a knowledgeable user. Photographers and photo enthusiasts are well aware of EXIF data and routinely use EXIF editors to make modifications to the data. Someone with criminal intent could easily alter EXIF data to change dates and times and/or GPS coordinates in an image file.

Obtaining EXIF Data from Facebook with a Legal Demand

EXIF data about images uploaded to Facebook is removed by the company. This is done to increase the privacy of the user by preventing other people from viewing the EXIF data of an image. Facebook also reports that by removing EXIF data it reduces the size of the image file and decreases the storage demands for multiple images.

However, just because Facebook removes EXIF data from images when they are posted it does not mean this information is no longer available. Facebook will divulge EXIF data and a duplicate of the originally uploaded file if a legal demand submitted to the company includes specific language those items.

Camera Make	LG Electronics
Camera Model	VS660
Orientation	0
Original Width	720
Original Height	0
Exposure	
Fstop	
Iso Speed	0
Focal Length	431/100
Latitude	34
Longitude	-85
Tags	

CORE SKILL: Viewing EXIF/Metadata

Viewing EXIF Data in Windows

Images shared via mediums outside of Facebook may still have the EXIF data intact. For example is a suspect sends pictures to a victim or an undercover officer. A simple way to check available EXIF data in Windows is to **right click** on the image, select **Properties**, and then the **Details** tab. This method works in Windows versions starting with Windows 7. It is not available for law enforcement officers whose departments have not upgraded from Windows XP.

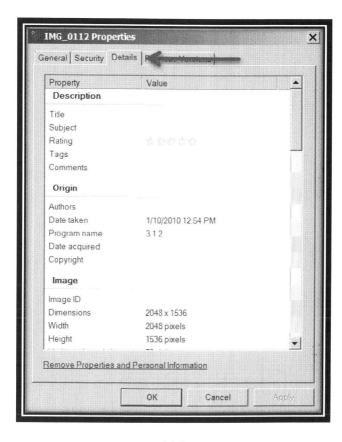

115

Examining the details of an image using Windows will show all available EXIF data including user descriptions or tags, origin, image information, camera type and settings, advanced photo features, GPS coordinates, and file attributes.

The downside to using Windows to view files is there is no way to easily export the EXIF data. Also, GPS coordinates need to be copied and pasted in a mapping service or software. This may not represent a challenge for a single image but can be a problem if looking at multiple images.

Using EXIF Viewer Software

Many law enforcement officers use free software programs for reading EXIF data such as Opanda. While Opanda is easy to use and can be downloaded as a portable application so it does not need to be installed on a department's computer, it does have some limitations. The primary consideration is Opanda and similar programs are not forensic. This means it is possible for data to be changed by the software program. This opens up potential defense attorney challenges if there is no way to prove the software did not make alterations to the image file. There are two good alternatives for working with images in a forensically sound manner while still getting EXIF data.

Forensic Image Viewer (FIV)

For investigators looking for a forensically sound method for viewing EXIF data Forensic Image Viewer (FIV) is a free software program from Sanderson Forensics, a civilian forensics company in England. The software has a number of useful features including an easy to navigate interface and automatic integration with Bing's mapping tool to instantly plot GPS coordinates found in the EXIF data. FIV also has basic image enhancement tools and keeps of log of all actions taken with a digital image.

Naturally, there are some drawbacks to the software. While Sanderson Forensics markets other paid forensic tools, FIV is offered for free. As such there is no support for those who encounter problems. FIV does not appear to have been updated in several years but it still works. The company also has a very cumbersome processes to download the software. Those who wish to use the software must register for the company's forum which requires completing a sign-up form and answering a basic computer forensics question before receiving a confirmation email that must be clicked to activate the site.

Once downloaded and installed, use the **Browser** tab to navigate to the image files.

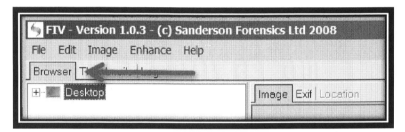

Next use the **Thumbnails** tab to select the image.

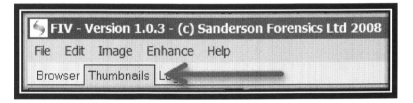

Double clicking an image will bring up another tabbed interface at the top. Select **Exif** to view the information about the picture.

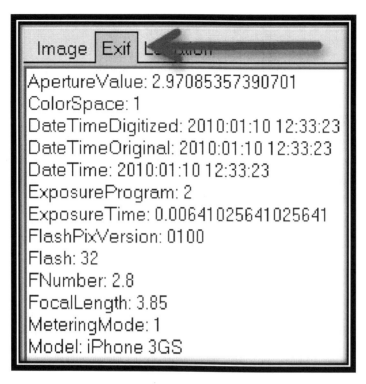

Selecting the Location tab brings up Bing Maps to view the GPS coordinates if they are encoded in the image.

FIV comes with some basic image manipulation tools found in the **Image** tab and a file of all actions taken with the image in the **Log** tab.

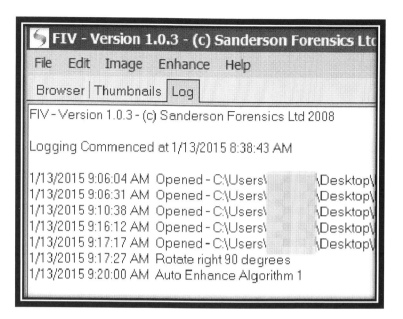

An important note about the log file information is that once the program is closed the logs are reset. Any documentation about what was done to the image are lost. Make sure to copy and save the information from the log file before closing FIV.

PictureBox

Another solid forensic tool for viewing images comes courtesy of Mike Harrison from the Kent Police in England. Mike develops and offers a variety of free forensic tools from his website mikeforensictools.co.uk. One of the tools he developed is PictureBox, which has several advanced features for EXIF examination.

The software can be downloaded and installed on a local computer. However, this requires Administrator rights on a departmental computer.

The main interface window is clean and easy to use.

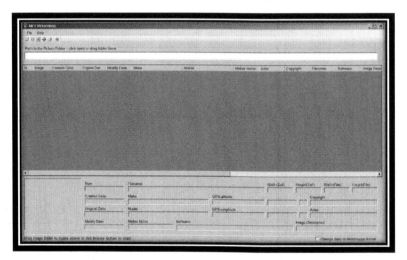

To examine an image's EXIF data either select the folder icon in the top menu bar or simply drag and drop the image into the white bar.

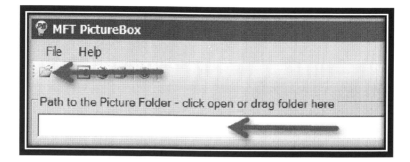

Next select the green arrow icon to run the process.

Once the process is complete the main window will display a thumbnail of all images in a file folder with the EXIF data in the columns to the right.

N...	Image	Created Date	Orginal Dat...	Modify Date	Make	Model
13...		2013:10:18 08:...	2013:10:18 ...	2013:10:18 ...	Apple	iPhone 5
13...		2013:10:18 08:...	2013:10:18 ...	2013:10:18 ...	Apple	iPhone 5
13...		2013:10:18 08:...	2013:10:18 ...	2013:10:18 ...	Apple	iPhone 5
13...		2013:10:18 08:...	2013:10:18 ...	2013:10:18 ...	Apple	iPhone 5

Selecting an individual image reveals the details of the image in a single interface.

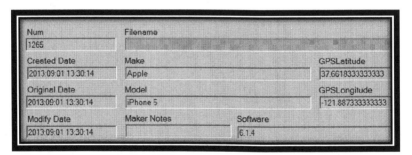

While there is no one-click interface to a mapping program, the GPS data can be exported as a KML file which can be viewed in Google Earth or other mapping service that accepts KML files. PictureBox has functions to export all of the EXIF data into an Excel spreadsheet or printed directly from the **File** menu.

122

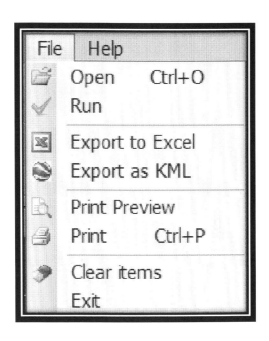

Metadata from Videos and Documents

While some investigators are aware of EXIF data in image files they may not know similar information exists in other file types. If a Facebook user sends a video or document outside of the social media channel there may be recoverable metadata from the file. Specific to videos taken with an iPhone or iPad it may be possible to recover the GPS coordinates where the video was taken. However, this data is not readable by most EXIF programs as the data is not in the EXIF format. The same applies to documents and other file types so a more universal metadata reader is required.

EXIFTool by Phil Harvey is a free tool that, despite the name, reads a number of different metadata formats. The software is available at http://www.sno.phy.queensu.ca/~phil/exiftool/. There are a few considerations before using EXIFTool. First, the software is not designed as a forensic tool. It is possible to change metadata in a file using EXIFTool. But, outside of expensive forensic programs there are not many alternatives for viewing EXIF data. Second, EXIFTool comes as a command line program which means there is no graphical user interface (GUI) for easy navigation. This can be challenging for law enforcement officers who are not familiar or comfortable with using the command line. Fortunately, another developer has created GUI that makes using EXIFTool very easy.

To get started you will need to have downloaded and unzipped EXIFTool from the website. Next you will need to download the GUI package from http://u88.n24.queensu.ca/~bogdan/. Depending on the operating system you may see one of two files **exiftool(-k)** or **exiftool(-k).exe**. In order for the GUI to work the original file name needs to be changed.

If the downloaded file is **exiftool(-k)** it needs to be renamed **ex-iftool**. Right click on the file and select **Rename**. Change the file name to **exiftool**. Do not add the .exe extension or the GUI will not recognize the program.

If the downloaded file is **exiftool(-k).exe** rename the file ex-iftool.exe. Keep the .exe extension but remove the other charac-ters.

The GUI should be placed in the same folder as EXIFTool. Next select the ExifToolGUI icon to launch the program.

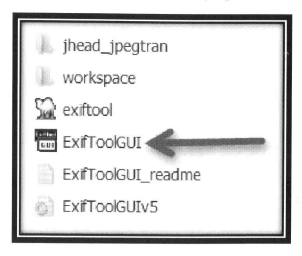

Once the program is running use the Browse tab to locate the files to be examined.

The middle pane of the GUI will show all of the files in the folder. A .MOV file is an Apple Quicktime movie file taken or used by an Apple device.

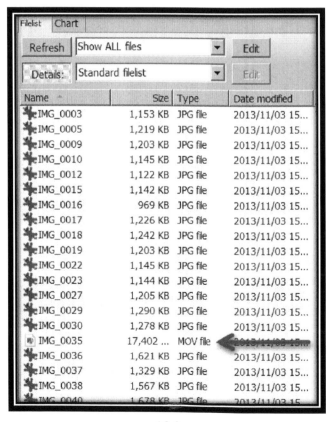

126

Selecting the **All** button on the right hand pane will display all of the available information.

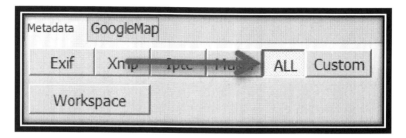

In addition to technical data about the file, the metadata available from a movie file may include the date and time it was created, the make and model of the device used to make it, and the GPS coordinates of where the device was when the movie was created.

ContentCreateDate	2013:09:01 13:07:24-07:00
GPSCoordinates	37.661500° N, 121.887000° W, 104 m Above Sea Level
Make	Apple
HandlerType	Metadata Tags
Make-und-US	Apple
CreationDate-und-US	2013:09:01 13:07:24-07:00
GPSCoordinates-und-	37.661500° N, 121.887000° W, 104 m Above Sea Level
Software-und-US	6.1.4
Model-und-US	iPhone 5
CreationDate	2013:09:01 13:07:24-07:00
Software	6.1.4

127

EXIFTool and the EXIFTool GUI are not limited to images and movie files. They can be used to examine metadata in other file types such as PDF files and Word documents. While there is no location data, it may still be possible to find information such as who authored the document and who modified it.

FileType	DOC
MIMEType	application/msword
	---- FlashPix ----
CodePage	Windows Latin 1 (Western European)
Title	E-mail search warrant go-by
Subject	
Author	
Keywords	
Template	Normal
LastModifiedBy	
RevisionNumber	3
Software	Microsoft Office Word
LastPrinted	2013:09:30 18:43:00
CreateDate	2013:09:30 19:06:00
ModifyDate	2013:10:18 20:52:00
Pages	15
Words	3320
Characters	18926

Reverse Image Searches

Images posted to Facebook may exist elsewhere on the Internet, including other social media websites. Images may also be copied or downloaded from Facebook and sent via other methods such as email. Identifying other locations where these images have been posted or where they came from can provide valuable investigative leads.

For example, assume the image of the Northern Hispanic gang member illustrated below was recovered during a forensic examination of a suspect's phone. Identifying other locations the image appears could provide leads to the identity of the subject in the picture.

It is possible to do a reverse image search using Google Images. From the Images main search page click on the camera icon to the right of the search bar.

For when family trivia nights get competitive, there's the Google app

In the tabbed interface select **Upload an image** and navigate to where the image is stored using the Browse feature. Once located select **Open** and Google will search the Internet for other locations where the image can be found.

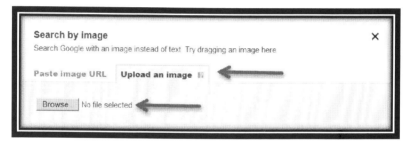

The reverse image search shows the example can be found at https://www.facebook.com/norte.cali14/photos/a.391459127610227.95364.391385050950968/4637292770 49878/?type=1&theater

Investigators familiar with California gangs will note the Facebook page is for Norteno (Northern Hispanic) gang members.

Finding one image on Facebook may lead to other social media suchs. An image may be posted across multiple social media sites including Facebook, Instafram, and Tumblr.

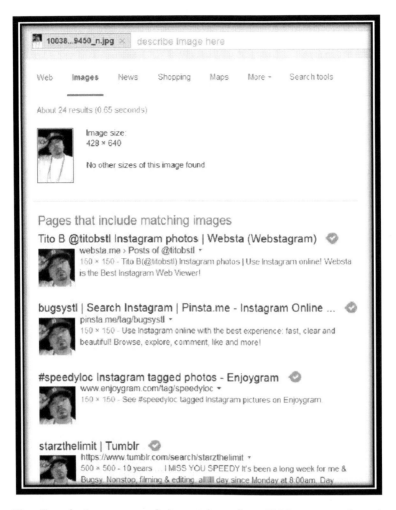

The Google Image search is not based on EXIF or metadata. It looks for the characteristics of the image. While many times it will find the exact match, there may also be irrelevant search results.

An alternative to Google's Image search is www.tineye.com. This site offers a reverse image search. The results are not always as good as the Google Image search but checking multiple search engines can provide investigative leads that might be missed by only checking one.

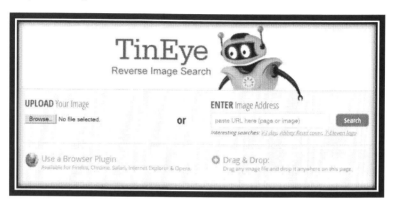

Decoding Facebook Image File Names

When an image file is uploaded to Facebook the company strips the EXIF data and the file name given by the user of created by the device that took the picture. Facebook assigns a new, unique file name to the image. It is possible to search for the page the picture was downloaded from, even if the profile is locked and not publicly viewable.

For example, assume the image below was downloaded and sent to another party. To determine where the photo originated it is necessary to examine the file name. Facebook renamed the file 1209250_545047268898124_822426277_n. The unique identifier for the picture is middle series of numbers separated by the underscores. In this case 545047268898124.

To resolve the image to a Facebook account it is necessary to do a specialized search. In the URL bar of any Internet browser type graph.facebook.com/ followed by the picture ID number. In this example the URL in the web browser would be entered as graph.facebook.com/ 545047268898124.

The results show the picture was posted on the website of the Fremont, CA Police Department and lists their Facebook ID. If this profile was locked and related to a crime the investigating officer would still be able to serve Facebook with a preservation letter of legal demand without needing to view the page.

```
"id": "545047268898124",
"created_time": "2013-10-09T22:18:24+0000",
"from": {
   "category": "Government organization",
   "category_list": [
      {
         "id": "161422927240513",
         "name": "Government Organization"
      }
   ],
   "name": "Fremont Police Department",
   "id": "207387302664124"
```

Free Facebook Search Warrant Template and Non-Disclosure Order

A digital format of the sample preservation letter and search warrant language can be obtained for FREE from https://gumroad.com/cipublishing. Simply select the appropriate template and put $0 in the checkout box and the files can be downloaded to your computer.

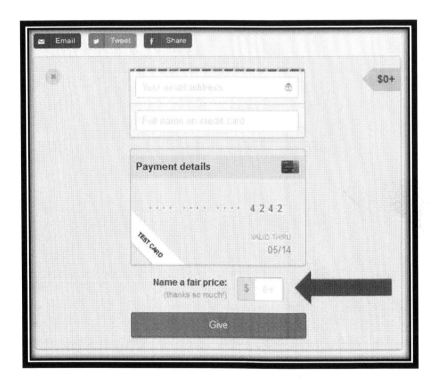

You might also be interested in:

ONLINE INVESTIGATIONS: Craigslist

How to find narcotics, human trafficking, explosives, stolen military equipment, fencing operations and more using specific keywords and search terms

Undercover operations: Tools and techniques for effective operations

Downloadable search warrant templates

ONLINE INVESTIGATIONS: Skype

Why investigators may be missing phone calls made using Skype

Recovering Skype evidence using free and paid tools

A search warrant template to recover Skype data

ONLINE INVESTIGATIONS: Snapchat

Are the messages really gone? A detailed guide to the information the company collects and retains and how to obtain it

Snapchat and mobile device search warrants to forensically recover Snapchat messages and log files.

64752842R00081

Made in the USA
Lexington, KY
18 June 2017